Drugs Info File

Dr. Miriam Stoppard

Drugs Info File

From alcohol & tobacco to ecstasy & heroin

DORLING KINDERSLEY
London • New York • Sydney • Moscow
www.dk.com

For Ed and Amie

A Dorling Kindersley book
www.dk.com

Senior Managing Editor	Corinne Roberts
Senior Managing Art Editor	Lynne Brown
Consultant Editor	Jemima Dunne
Project Editors	Dawn Bates, Debbie Voller
Editor	Claire Cross
Art Editors	Trond Wilhelmsen, Keith Davis
DTP Designer	Rajen Shah
Production	Martin Croshaw

First published in Great Britain in 1999
by Dorling Kindersley Limited, 9 Henrietta Street,
Covent Garden, London WC2E 8PS

A CIP catalogue record for this book
is available from the British Library.

ISBN 0-7513-0623-1

Reproduced by Colourlito, Italy
Printed and bound in Graphicom, Italy

CONTENTS

WHY THIS BOOK?

The aim of this book is to inform and educate children on the dangers of drugs. I don't believe in scare tactics, moral indignation or finger-wagging, and I find it as unrealistic to imagine a society without drugs as I do to imagine a society without alcohol or sex. My main concern is the welfare of children and, although we may never be able to eliminate drug use completely, I believe we can minimize the dangers of drug-taking by giving young people sound, honest, realistic information. Then the consequences for them and the community at large will be the least damaging.

What are dangerous drugs?

Children have an unerring instinct for inconsistency and unfairness and soon work out that both tobacco and alcohol can be just as harmful as many illegal drugs – the fact that one drug is legal and another illegal has very little to do with its actual dangers. For example, as a doctor, I can't say that cannabis is more harmful than tobacco, because it isn't. Any responsible person must be concerned with all forms of drug abuse among young people, but a discussion of drugs can't begin with cannabis, ecstasy, acid or even magic mushrooms. No, for legal and moral reasons it has to begin with tobacco and alcohol – still the major drugs used by teenagers and both legal.

Dispelling the myths

It's not surprising that many teenagers reject all information, good and bad, from adults on the subject of drugs. The messages are often exaggerated, false, sometimes ridiculous, but nearly always inconsistent with their own observations and experience. Teenagers are sensitive to double standards so the response "Do as I say, not as I do" will not go far in promoting abstinence on their part. In this book I've tried to avoid exaggeration and prejudgement and have re-examined the assumptions that are too often made about drugs. A realistic examination of drugs has to consider the following:

* despite possible dangers, most drugs induce some pleasurable feelings
* total abstinence may not always be a realistic goal
* the use of illegal substances may not necessarily mean abuse
* one form of drug use doesn't inevitably lead to more harmful forms
* understanding the risks of drug use will not necessarily deter young people from experimentation
* young people are capable of making responsible decisions about drugs.

Research

I've been lecturing, making TV documentaries and researching on drugs for over 20 years. As a mother myself, I felt it was important to speak directly to concerned parents as well as to potential drug users as part of my research for this book. The feedback from interviews and focus groups is reflected in the information given and the visual approach.

Drug use interests me as much as drug education. Most drug policies have been confined to education and although they may have influenced attitudes, they haven't necessarily altered drug use – a fact I'm painfully aware of every time I receive a letter from a drug user or worried parent. Ignoring drug use harks back to the time when policy makers thought sex education could ignore contraception.

Respect and truth

The "just say no" approach to drug-taking is based on the belief that our sons and daughters are incapable of making decisions about drugs and it implies that adults aren't interested in their opinions or experience. Well I do respect young people's ability to reason and use their own experience, which is why I discuss drugs in honest terms of harm to mind and body without relying on the law to separate what's dangerous from what isn't. My goal is to be scientific and even-handed, thereby separating real from imagined dangers.

THE JARGON

Addiction – *A condition that occurs when a person needs to take drugs to survive from day to day; also called dependence.*

Cold turkey – *Term used to describe the physical withdrawal symptoms experienced when suddenly coming off a drug; commonly used in connection with heroin withdrawal.*

Comedown – *How a person feels as the effects of a drug wear off.*

Cut – *Term used when dealers mix or "water down" drugs with other substances, for example, sugars like glucose and lactose.*

Dance drugs – *Stimulant drugs, such as ecstasy, that are commonly taken at clubs and raves.*

Depressant – *A drug that dulls the central nervous system, slowing down heart and breathing rates and making the user feel relaxed and drowsy.*

Detoxification – *The process of coming off a drug and getting it out of the body.*

Flashbacks – *A side effect of taking an hallucinogen whereby the hallucinations that occurred during a trip are relived some time later.*

Hallucinogen – *A drug that affects the brain and causes the user to "hallucinate", i.e. see, hear and feel things that aren't there.*

Hit – *The first dizzying sensation when a drug reaches the brain, common with the first cigarette or the first alcoholic drink.*

Joint – *A hand-rolled cigarette containing tobacco and cannabis; also referred to as a spliff.*

Munchies – *The hunger pangs that are experienced after smoking cannabis.*

Narcotic – *Drug that causes sleepiness, dizziness, numbness and possibly unconsciousness.*

Opiate – *A drug that dulls sensations and causes sleepiness. A natural opiate is opium, prepared from the opium poppy.*

Over-the-counter – *A drug that can be bought in a chemist without a prescription.*

Psychoactive – *Term used to describe the action of a drug that affects mood, perception and behaviour.*

Rush – *The first feeling of nervousness and anxiety from taking a stimulant.*

Sedative – *A drug that affects the brain, slowing down bodily functions and inducing sleep.*

Serotonin – *A chemical found in the brain that regulates mood.*

Set – *The mood a person is in when taking a drug.*

Setting – *Where a person is and who they are with when taking a drug.*

Sledging – *A life-threatening condition brought on by certain drugs or cocktails of drugs whereby the user is unable to move or talk, and may fall into a coma and die.*

Snort – *When a drug is lined up and then sniffed up through a nostril via a tube or rolled banknote.*

Speedball – *The practice of mixing heroin and cocaine, with potentially very dangerous side effects.*

Spiked – *When food or drink has had a drug added to it without the knowledge of the user.*

Stimulant – *A drug that affects the central nervous system, increasing heart-rate and blood pressure and making the user feel pumped up and energetic, and act loud. These drugs are also known as **uppers**.*

"Street" name – *Colloquial name for a drug.*

Trip – *The experience undergone under the influence of an hallucinogenic drug such as acid – sensations are intensified and perceptions altered. A trip can be "good" or "bad".*

Withdrawal – *The unpleasant symptoms a person experiences when they stop using a drug they're dependent on.*

Works – *Term used to describe the equipment needed to inject drugs.*

Wrap – *A carefully folded piece of paper that contains drugs like heroin, cocaine or amphetamine; also called a **bag** or **deal**.*

NATIONAL DRUGS HELPLINE 0800 776600

If you have a problem with drugs or simply want some information about drugs, you can call this helpline. This 24-hour service provides confidential counselling and advice. answers general drug queries and supplies leaflets and literature on drugs free-of-charge. There are also separate lines available for ethnic-minority languages.

WHAT ARE DRUGS?

drug, n. substance used in medicine or as a stimulant or narcotic.

Drugs are not new. Man has been experimenting with them for thousands of years for escapism and fun as well as for healing purposes, spiritual enlightenment and ritualistic ceremonies. People today are looking for exactly the same form of escape, but now there's a '90s twist with new refinements of time-honoured, mind-altering chemicals. Nowadays when most people use the word "drug" they're thinking of illegal substances like cannabis, cocaine, crack or acid. Some use the word "poisons" to describe illegal drugs in order to demonize them but then alcohol, aspirin and nicotine are poisons too. Even water "poisons" the body when drunk to excess.

Most young people see occasional drug use in the same way as alcohol – as part of normal life. Most describe it as something that makes them feel good and gets rid of inhibitions. In the main they're as responsible about drugs as they are about alcohol.

Legal drug use

You don't have to use the so-called "street" drugs in order to be a drug user. Tea drinkers and smokers are drug users too. Alcohol, the caffeine in tea and coffee and the nicotine in cigarettes are all drugs – and they're legal.

Drinking alcohol and smoking cigarettes cause far more deaths than the use of illegal drugs. In the UK every year there are around 120,000 smoking-related deaths and about 25,000 deaths attributable to alcohol (including the innocent victims of road traffic accidents that are caused by drink-driving), whereas there are probably under 2000 deaths a year attributable to the misuse of all types of illegal drugs.

So, how did drugs become street drugs?

The traditional use of the word "drug" refers to substances that are taken for medicinal reasons. In fact it wasn't until the 19th century that a distinction began to grow between "medical" and "recreational" drug use.

Some medicines prescribed by doctors, for example, barbiturates and tranquillizers, are just as harmful and/or addictive as some of the illegal street drugs and indeed find their way onto the streets. Various plants and household substances are also being tucked under the drugs umbrella if they're used in certain ways. A common wild fungus called the Liberty Cap (one of the "magic mushrooms") contains a chemical that causes hallucinations when eaten, and butane gas lighter refills and paint thinners give a quick, cheap, but dangerous buzz when sniffed.

Most illegal street drugs started life in the laboratory as legitimate, respectable medicines; the medical profession developed them as possible remedies for various conditions:
• ecstasy started life as an appetite suppressant
• LSD (acid) was discovered by mistake by a Swiss chemist in 1943
• it was hoped that heroin would prove to be a powerful non-addictive painkiller when it was discovered in 1874.

ORIGINS IN PLANT LIFE

Chemical refinement of plants produces some powerful drugs. Even though they have a "natural" source, it doesn't mean they're not harmful:
• heroin is one of a group of drugs from the opium poppy; this group includes painkillers such as morphine and codeine
• cocaine comes from the coca plant, and was used as an anaesthetic in ear, nose and throat surgery
• LSD (acid) comes from a fungus that grows on rye grasses
• ecstasy is a synthetic compound modelled on a substance found in nutmeg and oil of sassafras.

Drugs are pulled as well as pushed – in other words, people actively look for them because they WANT to try them. 1 in 10 London schoolchildren push drugs to their friends.

HERE ARE DANGERS FROM TAKING DRUGS

How long have drugs been around?

It's a safe bet that ancient man began to smoke plants as soon as he'd discovered fire; and long before the invention of modern mind-altering chemicals like acid and ecstasy, he'd certainly discovered some natural alternatives of his own.

False...
Once people start to smoke cannabis they'll become addicted or go on to hard drugs.
This is like saying that you'll become an alcoholic after a few drinks; it's patently untrue.

- Historical evidence suggests that people have been using cannabis for 8000 years; it was used by many early civilizations as a medicine for anything from anxiety to digestive problems, even period pains. Ancient Sumerian texts (from the Middle East) hailed the opium poppy as a "joy plant" 6000 years ago.

- The chewing of coca leaves by natives of South America dates back to at least 2500 BC. Bolivians still use coca leaves as a remedy for altitude sickness.

- Mescaline (from a Mexican cactus plant) and magic mushrooms – both of which can be hallucinogenic – were used thousands of years ago in an attempt to raise the consciousness and spark off some kind of cosmic "inner journey". Both substances are as central to mystical tribal rituals as ecstasy is to the rave experience.

KNOW THE FORM
Drugs come in many guises – from the obvious pill and powder to liquids, resins and household solvents.

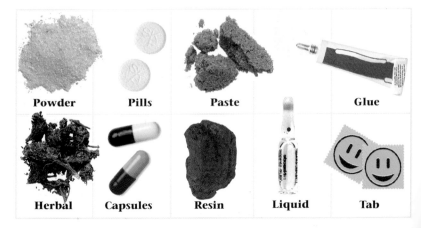

Powder	Pills	Paste		Glue
Herbal	Capsules	Resin	Liquid	Tab

Why do people take drugs?

Whether people are using fire, drums, chanting, flickering lights or music, their aims are the same – to escape feelings of isolation, and to feel a sense of unity with everything and everyone around them. The appeal of drugs has always been that they change the way people feel and how they perceive the world around them. People take drugs to:

- have fun and feel happy
- loosen up and be free of inhibitions
- feel confident and good about themselves
- be accepted by a group of friends
- feel sociable and enjoy people more
- forget ordinary life and relieve boredom
- forget problems and escape from worries
- enjoy music more
- enjoy dancing more
- stay up all night
- experiment and feel the thrill
- be rebellious
- relax and chill out
- reduce the effects of other drugs
- speed up the effects of other drugs
- ease "coming down"
- get some sleep.

True...
Many people who try drugs come to no harm*. Just as many adults naturally limit their drinking and smoking, many younger people will dabble only occasionally with illegal drugs.*
Tobacco is the gateway drug*,* ***not cannabis as is so often quoted.*** *Very few people smoke cannabis who haven't smoked cigarettes first – and cigarettes are legal.*

So, what's the problem?

A substance that's sufficiently active to change your brain chemistry, so that your perception is altered and you see the world differently, is bound to have serious after-effects. Everyone knows about the hangover after drinking alcohol. But people who drink alcohol are prepared to go for the short-term thrill and suffer the longer-term after-effects – that's the trade off. Other drugs are no different, they all trade an immediate high for a downer some time later.

WILL YOU OR WON'T YOU TAKE DRUGS?

You may know exactly how you feel about drugs. You may have seen friends getting high and decided that next time you get the chance you're going to try drugs too. Or you may be someone who hates the idea of losing control, so much so, that you're determined never to take drugs – even if it makes you feel like an outsider at times. Or you may be in two minds: sitting on the fence and weighing up the good and bad points, and wondering which way to jump.

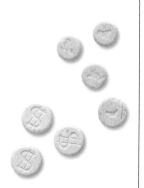

DON'T BE MISLED
The size of a tablet is not an indication of what it contains or how dangerous it may be.

Be well informed

The best way to explore your feelings about drugs is to find out everything you can about them, and arm yourself with the facts. Talk to people you trust: your best friend, your parents or the adult you get on best with. Share your feelings with older brothers and sisters if you have any. Get advice from a teacher whose opinion you respect, or from a social worker attached to your school. Try talking to people who have tried drugs and are willing to give you an honest account of their experiences – that means the lows as well as the highs. Take your time weighing up all the information and remember it's okay to say "No" whatever your friends say or do. Remember you always have a choice.

DON'T RUSH INTO AN

What to think about

There are some important facts to consider when you're thinking about drugs:

• you can go to prison if you're caught with illegal drugs

• drugs are extremely unpredictable – they can kill

• taking drugs is a leap in the dark – you can have as many bad trips as good ones

• drugs mess with your mind and body – one bad trip can leave permanent damage

• you always have to come down, and the higher you go, the harder you fall

• you can never be sure what's in a dose

• you can become dependent and/or addicted to many drugs

• if you're mentally unstable, drugs will make your condition worse; they can trigger mental illness.

SAYING "NO" TO DRUGS

If you don't want to take drugs, you can try saying things like:

"No, I can have fun without drugs."

"No, because I don't know what drugs might do to me."

Don't let anyone make you feel uncool just because you don't want to do drugs. You're cool if you stick to your guns. One of the most important things in life is being true to yourself.

If you really find it difficult to say "No", or you think your friends will laugh at you, you may find it easier to lie – try, "I can't take drugs because I'm on medication."

Remember you always have a choice.

The higher you go, the harder you fall.

Standing your ground

If you really don't want to do drugs:

• make some new friends who don't take drugs.

If your drug-taking friends try to make you feel like a freak because you won't join in, remember that there are plenty of other people who feel like you do

• avoid places where drugs are available

• focus on something positive that makes you feel really good about yourself, such as your studies or your favourite sport

• look after your body – exercise boosts self-esteem and gives you a natural high.

WHY PARENTS WORRY ABOUT DRUGS

When parents ask their children if they take drugs, they're looking for one answer – NO. Some parents don't even get as far as asking. They're not prepared to have any kind of discussion about drugs, except possibly to condemn them out of hand. This is a pity because there could well be a time when you need to talk about drugs to your parents, and not just because they've found out that you've been taking them. It may be that a friend has been taking drugs and you're worried about her health; or another friend may have been caught with drugs at home or at school and you're frightened about what may happen to him.

The strict approach doesn't work. Being really strict simply means people go to greater lengths to conceal what they're doing. It's human nature – anything that's forbidden is immediately attractive.

Take the initiative

Drugs may be the last thing you want to talk about with your parents, especially if it means admitting that you've taken them yourself. But for your sake and theirs, it's a good idea to try to take the initiative in starting a dialogue with them about drugs **before** there's a crisis. Your parents are concerned about your welfare so tell them what you know. Many parents only know scare stories about widely publicized drug-related deaths and jump to the conclusion that so-called soft drugs inevitably lead to hard drugs or believe that all illicit drugs are more harmful than tobacco and alcohol. Parents worry about drugs for all sorts of reasons:

- they fear for your safety and health
- they fear legal repercussions
- they are prejudiced
- their view is distorted by media reporting
- their moral and religious beliefs.

If your parents are very rigid in their thinking, you may feel inclined to abandon attempts at reasonable discussion and honest behaviour. Try to resist this because you'll both lose out in the long run.

EDUCATE YOUR PARENTS

Some adults are probably as confused and ill-informed as some young people.

- Show your parents the drugs education material you get from school.
- Show them books about drugs (including this one).
- Give them leaflets about drugs from nationally recognized agencies such as the Health Education Authority.

COMMUNICATION

By sitting down with your parents and having a sensible discussion about drugs, you may prevent unnecessary worry, misunderstandings and heartache.

If you've taken drugs

Let's face it, even if you've discussed drugs in a general way in your family, all parents are going to be alarmed if they find out that you've actually used an illegal drug – and some will be upset if they find out that you've been smoking or drinking, especially if you're under-age.

How your parents feel generally about drugs will inevitably colour their reaction. You can't blame them – parents always worry about their children, even when the children are grown up and have left home. Parenthood is a lifelong commitment! Try to put yourself in their position and think about how you'd react in a similar situation.

How concerned parents might react to you taking drugs

If your parents can talk to you about controversial subjects, you might expect:

Concern "Do you really know what you're taking?" "You would let me know if you get a bad reaction, wouldn't you?" "All we ask is that you're careful." "Why do you feel you need to take drugs?"

Disappointment "Well I hoped I'd never have to face this." "Well I can't say I'm happy about it."

Fairness "I'm concerned about it, but if you asked for it, I can't blame your friend for giving it to you."

Questioning "Well you've made this decision, but have you thought about the consequences?" "Do you really understand what could happen if something goes wrong?" "You do realize that it's illegal?"

Help "You can rely on us if you need help." "If there's a problem, please come to me first." "Don't feel you have to hide anything if you're in trouble."

If your parents can talk to you about drugs like this, you can all continue to be friends and be open, sensible and honest. Then perhaps you can make certain promises that will greatly allay their fears. You might promise to:

• find out the truth about drugs
• only take drugs when you're with good friends
• be careful with drugs
• never mix them, even with alcohol
• know what to do in an emergency
• understand the legal implications.

In return, get your parents to agree that if *you* find out the difference between the myths and realities of drugs *they* will too.

False...
Teenagers get into drugs through mixing with the wrong sort. There is no wrong sort. Growth in drug use includes people from every social class, ethnic origin and religious background.

SHOW YOUR PARENTS THIS

Rather than being judgemental and heavy-handed, there are really practical things you can do to help your children:

• learn about drugs and help your child to learn about them too
• think carefully about your views on drugs, and be honest with yourself and your child about your own drug use past and present – be it alcohol, nicotine, tranquillizers or cannabis
• don't be authoritarian: you'll lose your child
• know where to get help if it's ever needed
• keep drugs in perspective.

IF A CHILD REALLY WANTS TO TRY DRUGS, THERE

If parents over-react to you taking drugs

If your parents are badly informed or overbearing, you might expect:

Shock or anger "That's it, you've blown it this time!"

Over-reaction "You'll become an addict!" "You could overdose and die!"

Disbelief "What do you think you're doing?"

Guilt and shame "Where did we go wrong?" "What if the neighbours find out?"

Self-pity "How could you do this to me?"

Rows and ultimatums "No child of mine..." "While you live in my house..." "I'm stopping your allowance now!" "We're going straight to the police."

Abuse "You're useless, worthless." "That's it – you'll never get anywhere now."

Denial or an attempt to blame someone else "Not my daughter – I expect your friend made you do it." "I don't want to listen to any more of this."

What you can do

Try to understand why your parents are upset. Put yourself in their position. Try to explain your reasons. Remember, their reaction is probably mainly due to fear and guilt – and they'll need help coming to terms with the situation too.

• If they can't understand or refuse to listen, go to another sympathetic adult – a teacher, youth worker, older brother or sister, friend's parent, another relative, your GP, or a drugs counsellor – to try to get them to intercede on your behalf.

• Storming out of the house and threatening never to return doesn't help because it tends to harden attitudes, but if you think it would help everyone to have a breather from the conflict, find out if you can go and stay with someone close by for a few days to clear the air.

IF YOU'VE LEFT HOME

Keep phoning your mum and dad even if they put the phone down on you – do it for yourself not them – you'll feel better if you do. If you really don't want to stay directly in touch with your parents, stay in contact with someone in the family or a friend, so that at least your parents know you're all right. If you really don't know what to do, try phoning the Citizens Advice Bureau or the National Drugs Helpline, Release, Kidscape or even the Samaritans. All these numbers are on pages 124–5 of this book.

However upset or angry your parents may seem, underneath it all they're almost certainly worrying about your welfare.

DRUGS

AND THE LAW

Even though drugs are everywhere, it's still against the law to have or take most of them. Legal control of drugs began in 1868 and it's been getting tighter ever since. If you're considering taking any sort of drug, you should be aware of what can happen. Each year tens of thousands of people are arrested for drug offences. In 1996, over 72,000 people were found guilty of cannabis possession in the UK alone. Sentences for drug offences do vary depending on how harmful the drug is and the offence, whether it was for yourself or for supplying to others.

Tougher laws would only send drugs deeper underground, therefore increasing crime and violence.

Drug laws

There are two main laws in the UK covering drugs:
• The Misuse of Drugs Act 1971
• The Medicines Act 1968
The Misuse of Drugs Act controls the *use, production* and *supply* of all the drugs that are considered dangerous. These are called "controlled drugs" and they're divided into three "classes": A, B and C. Within each class the drugs are divided into schedules depending on whether they have any medical use. Penalties for taking or possessing any of these drugs vary a great deal depending on the drug, your personal circumstances (for example, your age and whether or not it's your first offence), but the maximum penalties are very severe.

IF YOU GET A CRIMINAL RECOR

The Medicines Act controls the way all medicines are *made* and *distributed*, which put simply means that if you have a valid doctor's prescription or you get a medicine from a pharmacy it's legal to have and to take the drug. However, it's illegal to supply it to another person or to make it without a licence. Drugs covered by the Medicines Act are substances such as amyl nitrite (one form of "poppers"), GHB, ketamine and some tranquillizers.

Criminal record

If the police catch you with illegal drugs on your person, or in your home or car, you can be prosecuted, even if you aren't actually using them yourself. If prosecuted and found guilty you get a criminal record – ask yourself whether you want this.

DID YOU KNOW?
- Criminal records stay with you for the rest of your life.
- If you've got a criminal record it can be more difficult to get a job.
- There are a lot of countries, including America, Australia and places in the Far East, that may never let you in if you've got a criminal record.

- **Class A drugs** are the most dangerous and include drugs such as heroin, cocaine, crack, LSD (acid), ecstasy and any Class B or C drug that's been prepared for injection.
- **Class B drugs** are slightly less dangerous and include amphetamine, some barbiturates and tranquillizers, cannabis and even codeine.
- **Class C drugs** include some benzodiazepine tranquillizers, such as temazepam, some barbiturates and anabolic steroids.

MAXIMUM PENALTIES UNDER THE MISUSE OF DRUGS ACT

Possession	Possession with intent to supply	Supply
Class A 7 years jail plus fine	Class A Life imprisonment plus unlimited fine and seizure of drug-related assets	Class A Life imprisonment plus unlimited fine and seizure of drug-related assets
Class B 5 years jail plus fine	Class B 14 years jail plus fine	Class B 14 years jail plus fine
Class C 2 years jail plus fine	Class C 5 years jail plus fine	Class C 5 years jail plus fine

'LL STAY WITH YOU FOR LIFE

REMEMBER, if the police can prove that an illegal drug has been in your pocket, handbag, home or car, you can be done for possession.

INTENT TO SUPPLY
If you're found with a drug such as cannabis that's been cut into pieces, you may be charged with intent to supply.

What are the main offences?

Possessing a controlled drug

In other words, you're found with a small amount of an illegal drug for your own use. This is viewed as the least serious offence. The more you have, the more suspicious the police will be about whether it's for your sole use – and there's no set amount below which they decide that it's for your sole use – it's up to them.

Possession with intent to supply others

This doesn't just mean intending to supply for money ("dealing"). If the police consider that you've got more of a drug than you need for your own use, and in a form that makes it easy to supply, they'll charge you with intent to supply. For instance, with one ecstasy tablet, you'll be done for possession, with two you could be arrested for supply even if they're both for yourself. If you've got a chunk of cannabis resin in one piece you may only be arrested for possession, but if it's cut into 20 pieces, even if it's still for you, you're more likely to be arrested for intent to supply.

Supplying drugs to another person

As with "intent to supply", the law doesn't make any distinction between sharing, giving away or selling. It's an offence to give away a single ecstasy tablet, or even to pass a joint to a friend.

Other offences

You can also be prosecuted for:
• unlawful production of a drug, which includes growing your own cannabis plants
• allowing your premises to be used for production or use of drugs, so if your flatmate is caught growing and smoking his own cannabis, you could be arrested as well. Or if you grow it at your parents' house they could be arrested
• offering to supply a drug even if you don't have any and have no intention of getting it
• supplying or offering to supply any equipment that can be used to administer a drug
• importing any drug into this country

IF YOU'RE
ARRESTED

If you become involved with the police your first reaction may be to mouth off and become stroppy or aggressive, even if you know you're innocent. DON'T – it'll just make the situation more difficult to deal with. Stay calm, keep quiet and ask for a solicitor. There are strict limits on how long you can be detained in a police station. If you're 17 or under, the police must contact your parents or guardian; you shouldn't be questioned without an appropriate adult present because the interview wouldn't be allowed as evidence in a court. If your parents do come to the police station and take responsibility for you, you're far more likely to be cautioned. If your parents don't come, you'll probably be charged with an offence.

CLASS A DRUGS
Ecstasy, heroin and cocaine are all
Class A drugs

Giving to friends
= Dealing
= Go to jail

Buying for friends
= Dealing
= Go to jail

Selling for profit
= Dealing
= Go to jail

Getting a solicitor

Whatever your circumstances, you're entitled to legal advice at the police station.

• Good legal advice can often mean the difference between being cautioned and being charged; or being charged with straightforward possession rather than possession with intent to supply.

• If you don't have a family solicitor, the police will organize a Duty Solicitor to attend free of charge. These aren't "police solicitors", they're local solicitors who take it in turns to advise suspects who don't have their own solicitor.

• Try not to be pressured into making any sort of statement until a solicitor arrives.

YOU GIVE AWAY A DRUG TO A FRIEND

THE RIGHT TO REMAIN SILENT

If you're arrested, you don't have to answer questions or give explanations, especially if there isn't a solicitor present. This is called the Right to Remain Silent. However, the Right to Remain Silent was amended by the Criminal Justice Act of 1994, so if you do refuse to answer questions, and you're later charged with an offence, the court can now take your refusal to answer into account when deciding whether you're guilty or innocent.

Getting a caution

If the police consider that your offence is relatively minor, and particularly if you're young and it's a first offence, they can give you an official "telling off", known as a caution. It's given by a police inspector in a police station and if you're 17 or under it must be done in the presence of your parent or guardian. Different police forces have different attitudes to cautioning, so you can't rely on it as an option.

Originally aimed at young people, cautions are now also used for adults. You can be cautioned more than once, but you're unlikely to be cautioned more than three times – after that you'll be sent to court.

The advantages of a caution are:
• you don't have to go to court
• the whole process is done relatively quickly, often within a few hours of the arrest
• although it's recorded officially by the police, and would be referred to in the event of a later arrest, it's not recorded as a conviction, and it's wiped off the record after five years
• it isn't usually made public.

The disadvantages of a caution are:
• you have to admit that you're guilty of the offence
• it's generally only used for the least serious offences, such as possessing a small quantity of cannabis for personal use.

If you're found guilty

If you're prosecuted and found guilty, sentences vary according to:
• the nature of the offence
• how harmful the drug is
• your personal circumstances, such as how old you are, and whether it's a first offence. The maximum sentences are only imposed in very serious cases.
Whatever happens you get a criminal record for life.

HANDLING DRUGS WITH COMMONSENSE

You may have friends who have experimented with illegal drugs like cannabis or ecstasy, and you may be interested in trying them yourself. But there are serious dangers associated with taking any drug. If you're determined to try a drug, don't do it without knowing what to expect – the downside as well as the upside.

PSYCHEDELIC SPECTRUM

PURE STIMULANT

Amphetamine

Cocaine

**Ecstasy, MDMA
MDEA**

MDA

Acid

PURE PSYCHEDELIC

These drugs share actions on a spectrum from purely psychedelic (acid) to purely stimulant (amphetamine), with ecstasy in the middle having both.

What drugs do

Loosely speaking drugs have four different kinds of effect on the body:

• stimulants (such as amphetamine) quite literally speed up the body
• depressants (such as alcohol) slow the body down
• hallucinogens/psychedelics (such as acid) alter the way people perceive the world around them
• narcotics (such as heroin) induce a feeling of passive drowsiness.

But not every drug fits neatly into one category. There's cannabis, which gives users a bit of everything: it relaxes, mellows and some of the modern blends can also trigger hallucinations. There are drugs such as MDMA (ecstasy) that are halfway between being pure stimulants and pure psychedelic/hallucinogens. In fact all the drugs in the ecstasy family fall somewhere on the psychedelic/stimulant axis; some are more psychedelic than stimulant and some are the other way around.

NOW THE FACTS ABOUT DRUGS

Know what to expect

• Most drugs with a **stimulant** effect produce a rush, and this is usually the first feeling. The most commonly experienced rush is from tobacco – that slight feeling of giddiness after the first puff of the first cigarette of the day. Or the "hit" from alcohol – 20 minutes after the first mouthful – the warmth behind the eyes, and in the legs. Not surprisingly, because of its name, a rush feels like a sudden burst of energy when everything inside your body and your head is whizzing, dizzying, fainting and swooning. Involuntarily you may start gasping for breath.

• With ecstasy and amphetamine the rush can make people want to dance and never stop. The rush from MDA (ecstasy's parent drug) can make people want to sit down in a cool place and take deep breaths – and they should do just that.

• **Depressant** drugs, including alcohol, dull the central nervous system so the heart beats more slowly and this can give people a feeling of well-being, relaxation and loss of inhibitions.

Mixing drugs is always a bad idea as each drug worsens the effects of the other and the risk of an overdose is real.

"The rushes kept coming and going and I thought, 'I'm going to die soon'."

"Suddenly my muscles went into spasm and I felt my body become rigid."

WARNING! If you don't know what you're taking you could easily overdose.

• Drugs with hallucinogenic effects take an hour or so to act and they change the way people see the world. The changes can be pleasant, such as colours seeming more intense; or they can be frightening, such as thinking you're being attacked by strange animals. These drugs can take hours to wear off.

• It's asking for big trouble to take any drug unless you're sure what it is and where it's come from. Drugs are often padded out (cut) or substituted with anything from caffeine, flour or glucose to dog-worming tablets, all of which can be very harmful. Sometimes a drug is cut with another drug; for example, ketamine is often added to ecstasy and has horrible, unexpected effects.

"I just couldn't breathe. I couldn't get air into my lungs. I knew I was suffocating."

You, your mood and your friends

How you'll react to a drug depends only partly on what's in it. But reactions to the same drug can also vary from time to time and in different situations. The "set", literally your mind-set (your mood) when you take the drug: whether you're happy, sad, up, down, nervous or relaxed may mean a good trip or a bad trip. Where you are and who you're with – the "setting" – can also affect you positively or negatively. If you're somewhere you don't like or with people who make you feel uncomfortable, you're more likely to have a bad experience.

WHAT'S A BAD TRIP LIKE?

A bad trip from ecstasy, speed, acid or strong cannabis can affect you physically and emotionally. The worst part is that you can get flashbacks for months, even longer, when you'll relive the horrors of the bad trip. Everyone's bad trip is different and hard to put into words but it's possible to build a mental picture afterwards.

Know the downside

You may know the pleasant and glamorous effects of certain drugs but do you know the negatives? Stimulants can cause overheating and dehydration. A "trip" may not go as you'd hoped – it could be nightmarish. And, remember, every time you go up you have to come down and the comedown can be nasty.

"The worst bit was the paranoia and terror. I thought it would never end."

"Coming down"

The feelings of exhaustion, depression and sickness (being wasted) that come on in varying degrees when a drug wears off are described as "coming down". And the higher you go, the harder you fall. With stimulants the high is achieved using up the body's own store of energy – the drug merely acts as the trigger – so a down is inevitable when exhaustion and depression hit and the down can last for several days. Persistent use of stimulants can cause prolonged and "deeper" downs as the body has less time to recover.

• The comedown after the frequent use of any drug can make you feel paranoid, jittery and panicky.

• After cocaine the comedown is a sudden, intense and deep blackness. The more cocaine you take to compensate the deeper you go.

• Ecstasy can leave you feeling low and apathetic for up to a week.

• Crack gives at best a ten-minute high, followed by a low that can last for days and has been described as "rolling down a hill of broken glass".

• Tranquillizers give people a terrible hangover.

Know how to look after yourself

The dance/drug combination can cause real problems. Dance drugs like ecstasy, amphetamine and acid are stimulants that go hand-in-hand with the all-night dance culture of clubs and raves. The greatest dangers of taking them are dehydration, heat exhaustion and heatstroke. Although dance drugs speed up your body, giving you the energy to dance for hours, dancing in a hot club makes you overheat and sweat to excess, depleting your body of water and salts. The problem with dance drugs is that you probably won't feel tired, thirsty or hungry until it's either too late or the drug wears off, even though your body is exhausted and dangerously low on minerals and water.

KNOW THE CLUB

A good safe club should have:
• free water
• water, high-energy drinks, fruit juice and salty snacks for sale
• chill-out areas
• lots of public telephones, with the local hospital phone number and a taxi number displayed
• a resident paramedic.

WARNING! Drinking too much water too quickly can cause the brain to swell, and lead to rapid death.

THE DANGERS

• If you take stimulants and dance all night, your body temperature may rise to over 40°C. If you can't cool down you may become delirious, develop heatstroke, fall into a coma and you could die.
• You may suffer body cramps, a splitting headache and vomiting.
• Your heart-rate may increase to a dangerous level. Long-term stimulant users risk heart failure and even young, healthy people are at some risk of a heart attack – the more you use, the greater the risk.

Safety

Follow these guidelines and you reduce the chance of meeting problems face to face: **Drink half a pint of liquid (NOT alcohol) every half an hour**
Stimulants naturally increase your body temperature. Taking them in a hot place, like a club, raises your body temperature even more. If you also dance for hours, your body temperature goes through the roof. You overheat and to try to counter this, your body sweats – buckets. You must replace these lost fluids with high-energy sports drinks, fruit juice or water. They help to restock lost minerals and vitamins as well as the water, so your body has a better chance of recovering from the pounding it takes during a night's clubbing.
• Don't gulp the drink all at once. Drink some about every 15 minutes.
• Never drink alcohol. It makes you even more dehydrated, and is a nasty additive to any other drug.

It depends on how much you sweat, but drinking more than three pints of water in an hour is dangerous.

Eat salted crisps or peanuts This helps your body to replace salt lost through sweating. If it's not replaced, the least you can expect is aching limbs the morning after.

Spend regular periods in the chill-out room These rooms aren't provided for decoration, they're there to allow your body to recover and cool down.

Don't wear a hat Hats keep heat in the body. You may think you look good wearing one, but you'll feel terrible as you're more likely to overheat.

Cool off with water If you're hot, splash water over your face and head.

Go with friends Your mood ("mind-set") will be better if you're with people you like, and you're more likely to look out for each other.

KNOW THE DON'TS
• **DON'T** take alcohol with drugs.
• **DON'T** take more drugs after the first dose.
• **DON'T** mix drugs – they can react with each other producing serious side effects.
• **DON'T** dance all night without having regular breaks, preferably outside or in the chill-out room.
• **DON'T** dance all night without drinking liquids.
• **DON'T** wear a hat.
• **DON'T** drive a car or use machinery.

True...
• *The majority of deaths from taking ecstasy could have been avoided if the users had known and practised the proper precautions – drinking a pint of water hourly and chilling out several times while out clubbing.*
• *Most teenage users have no problem growing out of the drugs phase.*

Know what to do in an emergency
Read the "If something goes wrong" section for each drug. This tells you what to do if you or a friend suffer adverse side effects. Also read the last chapter "What to do in an emergency" *(pages 119–23)* and, if possible, go on a first-aid course. **Quick-thinking friends have saved lives**.

Warning signs to watch out for:
• disorientation (the person can't say where she is or what day it is)
• drowsiness (the person is unresponsive to commands such as "Open your eyes")
• having fits (convulsions)
• gasping for breath or difficulty breathing
• feeling abnormally hot to the touch, even though the person's been in a cool environment
• fainting or unconsciousness.

If you notice any of the above, get help from a member of the club staff or ☎ **Call an ambulance. Always say what you think your friend has taken.**

drugs
directory

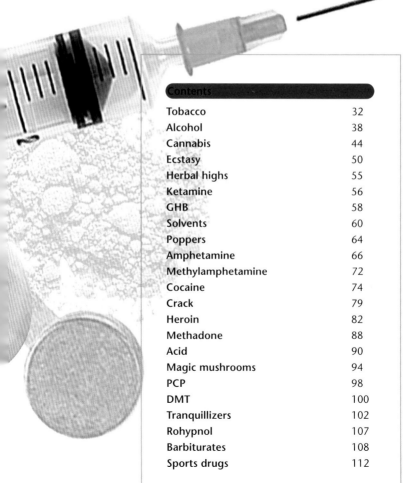

Contents

Brief history

British explorer Sir Walter Raleigh is credited with bringing tobacco to Europe from the New World in 1592. Raleigh saw how the natives dried, pressed and chopped tobacco leaves, then put them into pipes and smoked them for pleasure.

What is tobacco?

Tobacco leaves contain one of the most **powerful poisons** known to man – nicotine. A few drops of nicotine in its pure form when swallowed can kill in minutes. The nicotine hit is exceedingly quick. In cigarette smoke it's absorbed directly from the mouth and because the smoke is alkaline it dissolves instantly in saliva. It's then carried through the mouth's lining into the bloodstream and straight to the brain – the result is that you become dizzy and lightheaded in seconds. The nicotine in cigarettes and cigars is **physically and mentally addictive**, and with heavy, long-term use smoking tobacco eventually kills – through heart disease and lung cancer – more people than any other legal or illegal drug.

Tobacco

form

• The dried leaves of the tobacco plant are processed into tobacco for cigarettes, pipes or cigars.
• Tobacco is also sold as snuff, a fine powder that is sniffed.
• Tobacco sold in blocks is sometimes chewed, although it's rarely used in this country nowadays.

Rolling tobacco

Cigarette

Cigar

NICOTINE IS PROBABLY THE MOS

The nicotine effect

The hit from smoking a cigarette happens in seconds and lasts about half an hour.

• When nicotine reaches the brain, it makes the head spin. It makes people feel *stimulated* and *ALERT*.

• Nicotine makes the heart beat faster, so more blood circulates around the body per minute. People say they feel ready to get up and go.

• Nicotine reduces tension in muscles, which makes people feel r e l a x e d and **seems to relieve stress**.

• Nicotine seems to help people work by improving concentration. **It can stave off boredom and fatigue.**

Other names
Cigs, Fags, Rollies, Snouts, Tabs

IT'S THE INSTANT HIT FROM SMOKING THAT MAKES IT SO HARD TO RESIST

"Smoking my first cigarette was one of the most dangerous things I ever did."

Why people smoke

• To feel grown up.
• To feel **sociable**.
• To feel as if they belong.
• To feel cool.
• To feel smart.
• To feel like a rebel.
• It's **stimulating**.
• The cigarette feels **nice**.
• The lighter feels **nice**.
• The ritual of lighting up is pleasant.
• The first drag is *wonderful*.
• It's r e l a x i n g .
• For something to do with their hands.
• To look attractive and sophisticated.
• Eventually, because they're addicted.

"I felt awkward without a fag – embarrassed, tongue-tied, silly."

DDICTIVE DRUG YOU'LL EVER TAKE

Why it's so easy to get hooked

Smoking is not just an addiction – it's a ritual. Whether you smoke alone or with friends, have a leisurely cigarette or a quick fag break, it's the ritual itself that also becomes addictive. You might light up to be sociable, when you're nervous, or as an excuse to take a break. **There may be so many cues to light up that you end up smoking all the time**.

Here's a typical pattern of addiction:
- you start by having the odd cigarette to be sociable
- soon you begin to feel incomplete if you don't light up
- before you know it, you're smoking a pack a day and getting nervous as you get to the end of the pack
- then you go out late at night to buy more
- soon you can't bear to be without your cigarettes because **the ritual is as addictive as the nicotine itself**.

SMOKING MAKES YOU FEEL YOU BELONG

Q Surely I won't get lung cancer as long as I give up when I'm older?

A Only if you could be sure you would give up. Starting young exposes your lungs to that many more years of cigarette smoke, which increases your risk of lung cancer. Once you've got lung cancer, your chances of surviving longer than six months are very slim.

IF YOU HAVE TO SMOKE

DON'T smoke high-tar cigarettes. Stick to low-tar and keep your fingers off the tips.
DON'T smoke right down to the filter. This is where the cancer chemicals are concentrated, and if you leave a long stub you can limit the amount you inhale.

DON'T smoke more than five cigarettes a day if you can help it.
DON'T drink alcohol when you smoke or you'll soon find that you can't have one without the other.
DON'T add drugs to smoking.

IF YOU CAN RESIST SMOKING UNTIL YOU'R

Who's at risk?

You may be more likely to smoke if:

- your parents smoke
- your brothers and sisters smoke
- there are cigarettes lying around the house
- your girlfriend or boyfriend smokes
- your friends smoke
- people smoke where you socialize
- you don't care about the consequences.

WARNING! Nicotine is more addictive than heroin.

There IS a downside

Quite apart from the dangers of nicotine addiction and disease, the short-term effects of smoking aren't pleasant:

- you wake up *coughing*, and your mouth tastes like a drain
- you get **out** of *breath* easily, especially when playing sport
- nicotine stimulates the bowel and the bladder so you need to go to the toilet more often
- because smoking **dulls your taste buds**, eating isn't as pleasurable
- if you're a boy, smoking will make your erection limper and lower your sperm count
- it's **expensive**.

Why smoking NEEDN'T be attractive

If you think smoking makes you sexy and cool, **think again**:

- it makes your hair **smell**
- it makes your clothes **stink**
- it makes your skin **smell**
- your breath **smells** like an ashtray
- you're **horrible** to kiss
- your **face ages** more quickly.

Five women DIE every hour from smoking

Smoking and girls

More and more teenage girls are taking up smoking. Often influenced by images of models and film stars posing seductively with cigarettes, many young girls smoke a lot and eat little in the belief that they'll stay thin and "look cool".

You can give up

- 100 million people have given up.
- Don't let fear of failure put you off. Most people find it easier to give up than they'd imagined, and **those who fail at first do succeed eventually**.
- Most people wish they'd given up earlier.
- Giving up is one of the best things you can do for your body.
- If you're keen on playing sport, your body deserves to belong to a non-smoker.
- **Will-power** is the most effective way to give up, but you can be helped by products such as nicotine patches or gum.

WARNING!
Tobacco is THE gateway drug:
- most teenage drinkers smoke cigarettes first
- most cannabis users have smoked cigarettes first
- there are very few users of hard drugs who haven't smoked at some time in their lives.

The dangers of smoking

LUNG CANCER Years and years of smoking can cause lung cancer, but **it can be less than six months from diagnosis to death**.

FATAL HEART DISEASE Nicotine makes your heart beat faster and the carbon monoxide in cigarette **smoke robs the heart of oxygen**. The end result can be a heart attack. Nicotine can also cause constriction of the arteries, which raises blood pressure and causes heart attacks.

STROKE Because smoking makes your blood thick and sticky, it can't circulate properly. This means it will be more likely to clot. If you get a **clot in the brain**, you may have a stroke, which can mean permanent brain damage or paralysis, or even death.

THE END RESULT CAN BE HEART DISEASE

GANGRENE Your blood gets so sticky it can **block arteries**, which can lead to gangrene and, eventually, to amputation.

EMPHYSEMA AND BRONCHITIS Because the air passages in your lungs become clogged, narrow and damaged, you eventually become **crippled by breathlessness**.

OTHER SMOKING-RELATED DISEASES
- Cancer of the mouth, throat, oesophagus, bladder, pancreas, kidney, cervix and breast.
- Stomach and duodenal ulcers.
- Worsening asthma.

EVENTUALLY, NICOTINE KILLS MORE PEOPL

Smoking and pregnancy

• Mothers: don't smoke in pregnancy. A woman who does risks harming her unborn baby. It increases the likelihood of **miscarriage**, and of having an **underweight baby** vulnerable to infections.

• Fathers: research shows that the children of fathers who smoke 20 or more cigarettes a day have a **higher risk of cancer than children of non-smoking fathers**. Smoking damages sperm, so men should give up smoking at least three months before trying for a baby.

• Smoking increases the likelihood of **cot death**.

Q *But if I stop smoking, won't I gain weight?*

A *Possibly. But if you're tempted to snack, chew gum instead. If you do put on weight, don't worry. Anyone with the will-power to stop smoking can lose weight.*

The Law

It's not illegal to smoke at any age, but it's illegal for shopkeepers to sell cigarettes to someone who they know is under 16 years of age.

The rubbish in tobacco smoke

Up to 5 per cent of cigarette smoke is **carbon monoxide.** This is the same deadly gas that's in car exhaust fumes, and it stops your blood from absorbing oxygen properly. The same **tars** that are used to surface roads are in tobacco smoke, and can cause cancer. The most dangerous tar is a nitroso chemical: 1 part per billion in food is a hazard; in tobacco smoke there are 5000 parts per billion. The other chemicals inhaled include **ammonia** – a chemical found in explosives, bleach and lavatory cleaners, **cyanide** – a deadly poison, and **phenols** – a chemical used in paint stripper.

YOU INHALE OVER 3000 DIFFERENT CHEMICALS IN EVERY PUFF

What is alcohol?

Alcohol is **an intoxicating substance** made from fermented starches and, although it gives you an initial lift, it is actually a depressant drug. It slows down responses (affecting co-ordination) and the way the brain works (affecting judgement), so it makes people clumsy and **dopey**. It's one of the most widely used drugs, above and below the legal age limit.

Other names
Booze, Bevvies, Drink, Jars, Tinnies, Liquor

alcohol

What happens

Although it takes minutes for alcohol to reach the brain, it takes the liver an hour to break down the alcohol in a glass of wine or half a pint of beer.

• The less you weigh the more alcohol affects you, so there's a good reason for alcohol being illegal below a certain age. A slim teenage boy will get drunk far more quickly than a large adult male.

• A girl will feel the effects of alcohol faster and for longer than a boy.

The alcohol effect

Drinking alcohol makes people:

• feel like they're having more fun fun fun
• feel **CONFIDENT**
• feel r e l a x e d and calms their nerves
• feel able to open up and talk more
• let go and **lose their inhibitions**
• feel they fit in socially
• feel really happy and laugh more
• **forget their worries** for a while
• think they have the courage to overcome their fears.

Alcohol is addictive

WARNING! Alcohol is responsible for many, many more deaths than hard drugs.

ALCOHOL IS A DRUG LIKE ANY OTHER, AN

The downside

Drinking too much alcohol always has horrible effects.

• Drinking can make you **AGGRESSIVE** and violent. You're more likely to start arguments and pick fights.

• You become **unco**-*ordin*at*ed* and clumsy.

• Too much alcohol gives you double VisiON and *slurred speech*.

• Drinking when you're down can make you feel even more depressed.

• Alcohol is loaded with calories. It can make you **fat**, and it's bad for your skin.

• A bad *hangover* makes you feel really fragile. Your head pounds and you have an upset stomach.

• Alcohol can **damage a man's fertility and potency** (brewer's droop).

Some grim statistics

• Children – mainly girls – as young as nine are drinking themselves close to death.

• The number of young people admitted to hospital with **alcohol poisoning** has increased tenfold in the last decade.

• Nine out of ten boys under the age of 13 drink secretly.

• One thousand children under 15 are admitted to hospital with acute alcohol poisoning each year in the UK alone.

• One in four teenagers, especially boys, gets into **arguments or fights** after drinking alcohol. This could mean the police.

The Law

• *In the UK it's illegal to buy alcohol if you're under 18.*

• *A male is probably over the legal limit for driving if he's had two pints of beer, three shots of spirits or three glasses of wine; a female if she's had one pint of beer, two shots of spirits or two glasses of wine.*

• *Being drunk at a football match is also an offence.*

There's no magic cure for a hangover

BUT...
even though there's a legal limit, your personal safe limit may still be less, especially if you're of slight build.

WARNING!
You can still be over the legal limit next morning if you had a heavy drinking session the night before. There may be a legal limit for drinking and driving, but there's no SAFE limit.

IT'S DANGEROUS DESPITE BEING LEGAL

BE SENSIBLE

DO eat before you drink; even a glass of milk can help prevent a hangover.

DO drink twice as much still water as alcohol, and a pint of water before bed.

DO sip rather than guzzle when you drink alcohol.

DO avoid fizzy mixers and alcopops. The bubbles get the alcohol to your brain faster.

DO stay off alcohol completely for a few days after a party to let your liver get back to normal.

DO make a note of how much alcohol you get through in a week. Keeping a drink diary can be a real eye opener!

DO plan how you're going to get home before you go out. Book a cab in advance.

Mixing alcohol with other drugs

Mix alcohol with anything and you may vomit and become unconscious. If you're sick while you're unconscious, you could choke on your vomit and die.

Don't mix alcohol and other drugs

Mixing alcohol with ecstasy or amphetamines If you mix alcohol with these stimulants, you're likely to be very energetic and overheat. This will cause you to lose a lot of water and your liver will be unable to get rid of the alcohol so you're likely to become unconscious.

Mixing alcohol with methadone, heroin or tranquillizers You could go into a coma.

Know your limits

A unit is a half-pint of normal-strength beer or lager, a medium glass of wine or one measure of spirits. A relatively safe daily intake for adults is **2–3 units for women and 3–4 units for men.** But that's probably too much for an 18-year-old, let alone someone younger. However, no-one should drink every day. (This doesn't mean it's safe to save up the units you haven't drunk to binge drink your weekly allowance in one go!)

Know the strengths

Know how much alcohol you're drinking by looking at the ABV (alcohol by volume) on the label: ordinary beers and lagers are between 2 and 4 per cent ABV; alcopops are much stronger at between 4 and 5.5 per cent ABV. Because alcopops are sweet, you're likely to knock back too many, well beyond your limit.

STAY IN CONTROL – KNOW WHE

The dangers of alcohol

• If you drive after you've only had one drink, **you're still FIVE times more likely to have a car accident than someone who's a non-drinker**.

• Accidents are common with alcohol because **your reflexes are slowed down and you lose co-ordination.**

• You can black out or forget what you did for whole periods of time. If you wander off alone **you could pass out and choke on your own vomit.**

• Serious binge drinking can lead to fits, causing you to fall over, injure yourself and even lose consciousness.

• **You're more likely to get careless and have unprotected sex** if you're drunk, thereby risking becoming pregnant or getting a sexually transmitted disease.

• Alcohol has a high sugar content, so anyone with diabetes is advised to avoid it altogether.

• Drinking during pregnancy can cause foetal alcohol syndrome in your baby.

• Long-term heavy alcohol use leads to **physical dependence –** which means you can't do without it – and seriously **damages the heart, liver, stomach and brain.**

Alcohol is a powerful poison

DON'TS

DON'T be a secret alcohol drinker.

DON'T mix your drinks, especially strong ciders and lagers.

DON'T mix drink with drugs.

DON'T add smoking to drinking.

DON'T drink and drive, and never ride in a car driven by someone who has been drinking.

DON'T try to drink as much as your mates. It's not a competition.

DON'T think that drinking alcohol means you're grown up. It doesn't.

WARNING! There are times when even one drink may be too much.

Avoid alcohol if you're:
• taking any over-the-counter medicines – even cold cures (check the labels)
• taking prescribed or illegal drugs
• going to drive a car or ride a bike
• going to operate machinery.

Am I at risk?

You're more likely to become a problem drinker if:

- your brothers and sisters drink a lot
- your mum and dad go to the pub often
- your mum and dad drink a lot
- there's an alcoholic in your family
- your dad gets drunk and violent
- you've got low self-esteem – you think you're worthless.

WARNING!
People who drink secretly early in their lives are more likely to use drugs illegally.

Being sensible about alcohol

If you've been given small amounts of alcohol to taste at family meals you know what it feels like to drink alcohol and stay in control. A gradual introduction might be a sip of wine with food occasionally, wine diluted with water (half and half measures), or half a pint of shandy made with low-alcohol beer and lemonade (half and half measures).

> *"I felt sexy when I was drunk, but the next day I realized I'd just acted stupid and embarrassed myself."*

Drinking and sex

Because alcohol **lowers inhibitions**, many teenagers have sex for the first time when they're drunk. This often has **disastrous results**:

- both sexes get careless about contraception. This can lead not only to **unwanted pregnancy**, but also to HIV/AIDS, herpes and other **sexually transmitted diseases** (STDs)

Many teenage pregnancies are due to having unprotected sex while drunk

- it's hard to maintain an erection when drunk
- girls think boys' **love-making is fumbling and shambolic** when they're drunk.

Brief history

Wines and beers have been made from sugary and starchy plants since prehistoric times. One of the earliest accounts of wine-making was found on an Egyptian papyrus, dated 3500 BC. The ability to make spirits came much later – only about 1000 years ago. Since the 19th century, governments have been concerned about the effects of drinking alcohol, but have also found it a source of revenue – hence the high taxes on alcohol. When the US government banned all alcohol in the 1920s – "Prohibition" – drinkers were forced to indulge their habit in secret. Gangsters then took over control of alcohol distribution, just as nowadays large-scale dealing in illegal drugs tends to be controlled by criminals.

IF SOMETHING GOES WRONG

vomiting

If your friend needs to vomit, lean her forward so she doesn't choke. Give her water once she's stopped vomiting, and make sure she gets home safely.

Confusion

If your friend is confused and starts wandering off alone, stop him and make sure he gets home safely. If he passes out when alone, he could die of hypothermia or choke on his own vomit. If you are suffering from confusion yourself, get help.

unconsciousness

If your friend is breathing, place her in the recovery position (*see page 120*).

☎ **Call an ambulance.** Tell the medical staff what and how much your friend has been drinking.

• Be prepared to resuscitate your friend if she stops breathing (*see page 121*).

• If your friend vomits while unconscious, check that she's still breathing.

FITS

Ease your friend's fall if you can. Clear a space around him so that he can't hurt himself. Loosen clothing around his neck and put something soft under his head. When the fit stops, put him in the recovery position (*see page 120*).

☎ **Call an ambulance.**

If in doubt, phone the National Drugs Helpline 0800 776600

...UT DRUNK AND ALONE CAN BE FATAL

Cannabis

What is cannabis?

Most cannabis comes from a plant called *Cannabis sativa* that is mainly found in Asia and South America, although significant amounts are grown in North America and Europe. The most active chemical in cannabis – and the one that gets a person **stoned** – is called *delta9-Tetrahydrocannabinol* (THC). The amount of THC can vary greatly and cannabis that contains a high level can hit quite hard.

form

There are three forms of cannabis: herbal, resin and (the least common) hash oil.

Herbal
• The commonest form of cannabis, made from the dried leaves and flowers of the plant.
• Looks like the kind of coarsely chopped dried herbs used for cooking. It's usually a greenish-brown colour and has a sweet herbal smell.
• "Skunk" is a particularly potent strain that can have a markedly hallucinogenic effect.

Resin
• Made by compressing the sap on the leaves and stem into blocks.
• Colour varies from almost black through to a pale golden brown.

• Some forms of resin are hard and brittle, like charcoal, while others are as soft as liquorice. Resin is usually mixed with tobacco in a hand-rolled cigarette but, like herbal, it can be eaten when added to foods.

Hash oil
• Cannabis resin when dissolved in a solvent, filtered and allowed to evaporate, leaves a thick oil.
• Varies in colour from black to green, and smells strongly of rotting vegetables.
• It's either smeared on cigarette papers and smoked, but more usually it's mixed with tobacco and smoked.

Skunk can trigger hallucinations

CANNABIS CAN TRIGGER FLASHBACKS

Herbal

Resin

Hash oil

The cannabis effect

The effect that cannabis has depends on how often it's smoked, how recently it was smoked and how the body naturally reacts to the drug. It can make people:

• feel r e l a x e d , h^{a}p^{p}y and sociable, especially if they're with friends

• become talkative and lead them to think they have a "**deeper** insight" into the world, but they're more likely to be talking drivel

• lose their inhibitions and say and do things that are out of character

• find everything hilarious; even the smallest thing will set off the giggles

• get an attack of "the munChies" and want to eat lots of food, especially sweet snacks, such as chocolate or cake

• have heightened sensations so that materials feel softer and colours appear brighter.

The set and setting

Crucial to the effect of cannabis is how people feel when they take it – the mood or "mind-set" – and where and with whom they take it – the setting. Cannabis often exaggerates the way a person already feels. So someone who is chatty, happy and confident may feel even *more at ease*. Conversely, someone who feels d$_o$$_w$$_n$ and pensive may become more uncommunicative and depressed.

Brief history

There's evidence that people have been using cannabis for over 8000 years, mainly for medicinal purposes. Early civilizations saw cannabis as a possible cure for all kinds of ailments, from anxiety to leprosy. In the early 19th century, many pharmacies sold cannabis tinctures as over-the-counter treatments for pain; Queen Victoria's doctors gave her cannabis for her period pain. In the mid- to late 19th century, people began to use cannabis for pleasure – in fact, the drug was legal in the United States until the 1930s.

Street names for herbal
Marijuana, Grass, Dope, Draw, Puff, Blow, Weed, Gear, Spliff, Ganja, Herb, Wacky Baccy, Green, Bud, Skunk

Street names for resin
Hash, Pot, Dope, Shit, Black, Gold, Brown, Slate, Squidgy

Street names for hash oil
Honey, Oil, Diesel

AD TRIPS EXPERIENCED ON OTHER DRUGS

The Law
• *It's illegal to have, grow, sell or give away cannabis.*
• *While herbal cannabis and resin are Class B drugs, cannabis oil can be categorized as a Class A drug, depending on how it's produced, and therefore it attracts higher penalties.*
• *NOTE: It's a popular myth that there's a set amount of cannabis that will ensure you just get off with a caution. However, if you're found with a small amount of cannabis for your own use, you may only receive a caution.*

"I used to wake up in time to watch 'Neighbours'. One day it wasn't on. Turned out it was Saturday – I didn't have a clue. I decided there and then that it was time to lay off the puff, sort my head out and find out what life outside the flat was like."

Cannabis usage

Smoking
• Most users smoke cannabis on its own or mixed with tobacco in a hand-rolled cigarette, known as a joint or spliff. The smoke is usually inhaled more deeply and held down for longer than with a normal cigarette. There's no filter to catch the tar and if you're not used to this you'll probably have a prolonged coughing fit.
• Some people smoke cannabis in a pipe, called a "bhong", that cools the smoke before it's inhaled. Beware – using a bhong to smoke a stronger variety of cannabis may increase the effect and you could experience hallucinations and **impaired judgement.**

Joint

Eating
Some people add cannabis to foods, such as biscuits and brownies, to make hash-cakes or space-cakes. Beware of snacks at parties that may have been Spiked with cannabis.

WARNING! One high dose of cannabis can cause panic attacks.

Dangers

Cannabis stays in the body for far longer than alcohol – around two months.

• You may feel sober long before the effects have worn off. For four or five days after, you shouldn't operate machinery or drive as you're likely to have an accident in this state.

• Cannabis can **trigger mental problems** in people who may be predisposed to them.

• Cannabis is **risky for people with breathing problems**, such as bronchitis and asthma. Two spliffs is the tar equivalent of 6–10 cigarettes.

• Cannabis can **lower a man's sperm count**, and the sperm produced could be abnormal.

• As with smoking normal cigarettes and drinking alcohol, women who use cannabis risk **harming their unborn babies**.

• Some long-term, heavy users may get *panic attacks*, exaggerated *mood* swings and feelings of persecution.

Cannabis and alcohol

It's a bad idea to smoke cannabis and drink alcohol. The combination will dry you out and make you very unsteady on your feet; it can even make you violent. You are also more likely to feel sick or even be sick, especially if you haven't had cannabis before. The hangover from cannabis and alcohol can be a near-death experience.

Don't mix cannabis with other drugs

Mixing cannabis with ecstasy or speed is particularly bad because it can make you dangerously dehydrated. Nasty side effects from using cannabis with other drugs include hallucinations, being unable to move, having a heart attack and losing consciousness.

Effects that aren't so funny

• You may feel sick, dizzy and faint and this can hit you on the first drag or the last one.

• Your judgement will be impaired and you **lose co-ordination**.

• You can feel too **spaced out** to speak.

• Cannabis can dry you out, making your throat, tongue and lips **parched**; this is even worse if you drink alcohol as well.

• Time seems to come to a standstill; minutes can seem like hours, which can be unnerving.

• High doses, or even low doses of strong varieties, such as skunk, can lead to unpleasant **hallucinations**.

• You may feel *panic* or paranoia. The panic may be so extreme that you literally can't speak or move. You can't remember what has happened; this can occur with quite small amounts.

AD TO THE USE OF OTHER DRUGS

Myths and truths

There is so much conflicting information about cannabis. The scaremongers say it's dangerous, the pro-lobby say it's safe and beneficial. This profile will tell you THE TRUTH without the prejudices of different campaigners.

Does cannabis lead to harder drugs?

• Hardly ever. There's no concrete evidence that cannabis is the "gateway drug". **Tobacco is the gateway drug for most heavy drug users.**

• People who abuse hard drugs are usually psychologically damaged and probably would have escalated to hard drugs with or without cannabis.

• It's probably true to say that people who use cannabis are more likely to be in situations where they'll be offered other types of drug.

Does cannabis cause memory loss?

Cannabis can cause short-term memory loss after long-term or heavy use.

Can cannabis cause birth defects?

There's a strong link between smoking cannabis while pregnant and a baby having abnormalities, as well as stillbirth, miscarriage or early death of a baby. If a pregnant woman smokes cannabis, the drug enters the baby's body through the placenta. The baby feels the same effects as the mother, but to a much greater extent and is much more easily harmed. So **never use cannabis during pregnancy***. You should also give up cannabis for at least three months before trying to conceive – and that means both of you.*

Does cannabis cause brain damage?

At the time of writing there is no conclusive medical evidence either way. No-one knows the long-term effects of taking cannabis repeatedly over a long period, but prolonged heavy use of any drug is always undesirable.

Does cannabis cause cancer?

Because of its **high tar content** it's likely that smoking cannabis can cause cancer of the throat and lungs. This is, however, difficult to prove scientifically as most users who develop cancer also smoke cigarettes, and cigarette smoke is associated with several cancers.

Can cannabis be used to treat diseases?

It's very useful for treating Multiple Sclerosis (MS). Doctors prescribe a similar drug to treat MS, but sufferers don't find it as effective.

CANNABIS CAN BRING MENT.

Don't hide from your problems
Some people use cannabis as a way to ignore their fears and failings. When they emerge from their cannabis haze, they find that their problems are not only still there but that they loom larger than ever. Becoming unmotivated is a real risk, and shouldn't be taken lightly. **The only way to get through life is to face it, not turn your back on it**.

Is cannabis addictive?
• **Cannabis isn't physically addictive**. Your body won't crave it in the way that it would crave a drug such as heroin or tobacco.
• **BUT you may develop a "psychological habit"** if you use cannabis often, becoming convinced that you can't do certain things until you've had a spliff.
• Very heavy cannabis users may suffer psychological withdrawal symptoms; they may become *anxious*, even paranoid, and unable to sleep at night.
• If you're a heavy user, **cannabis can be a difficult drug to give up**. If you're struggling to give up cannabis, you must get help. Contact your doctor or phone the National Drugs Helpline for advice on 0800 776600.

IF SOMETHING GOES WRONG ▶

vomiting
If your friend needs to vomit, lean her forward so she doesn't choke. Give her some water once she's stopped vomiting, and make sure she gets home safely.

panic attack
If your friend is paranoid, anxious and starts to panic take him to a quiet room away from large groups of people and try to reassure him. Offer him some water, and keep talking to him. Don't let him wander off alone. If your friend begins panting (hyperventilating), get him to try to copy your breathing.

Bad trip
Your friend may begin to see or hear frightening things that aren't really there – this is known as hallucinating. This can be extremely frightening and may cause your friend to panic. Talk to her and reassure her that the things she can see or hear are imaginary and will soon pass. Stay with your friend until the bad trip is over – don't let her wander off alone.

If in doubt, phone the National Drugs Helpline 0800 776600

LNESS TO THE SURFACE

Street names

**E, Love Doves,
Clarity, Adam,
Disco Biscuits,
Shamrocks,
MDMA, X, XTC**

What is ecstasy?

The popular dance drug ecstasy is the chemical *Methylenedioxymethamphetamine*, or MDMA for short. It leads a bit of a double life because it's a **stimulant** (a relative of speed), with **hallucinogenic** tendencies. Ecstasy is described as an empathogen as it releases **mood-altering chemicals**, such as *serotonin* and *L-dopa*, in the brain, and generates feelings of love and friendliness – people feel "loved up" and "blissed out". Because it's also a hallucinogen, the world becomes surreal, highly coloured and distorted. But ecstasy makes people nice, not nasty.

ECSTAS

*Your heart pounds...
You feel faint...*

form

Ecstasy tablets come in different sizes and colours, and often have logos such as doves on them.
• MDMA may be "cut" with other rubbish, such as dog-worming pills or talcum powder, to bulk out the tablet. Powerful drugs, such as amphetamine, ketamine (an anaesthetic) or selegaline (used to treat Parkinson's disease), are also added giving horrible unexpected side effects.
• Even some "reliable brands" turn out to be fake; in fact only about one-third of all tablets sold contains enough MDMA for a "true" ecstasy experience. When different colour "doves" were analysed, one contained as little as 29 mg MDMA, another had as much as 170 mg, and one had none at all – it contained pure ketamine and was, therefore, very nasty.

**WARNING!
Be prepared
for an unusual
or unpleasant
experience.**

MORE THAN HALF AN ECSTASY TABLET COUL

The ecstasy effect

After about 30 minutes the effects begin. They peak in an hour and last for 2–3 hours:
• sensation is altered and the skin feels warm and tingly
• **life has never felt so good**. Perception is keen – light and colours are brighter and sounds are exquisite
• music seems louder and the beat more insistent – it seems to come from inside
• energy levels rise so people want to leap around and dance all night
• everybody loves everybody. People want to touch and hug, but not in a sexual way – **everyone feels part of a huge, happy group**.

Everything around you seems in perfect harmony...

WARNING! You can die from taking just one tablet.

Brief history

Ecstasy (MDMA) was discovered as long ago as 1912 in the United States. It was first used as an appetite suppressant, but when it was found to calm feelings of anger, marriage guidance counsellors used it to get couples to talk to each other. In 1988 the rave scene became popular and ecstasy took on a new role as the main dance drug.

The bits you might not like

A bad ecstasy experience is far from pleasurable:
• your heart pounds, you feel **sick** and you might even throw up
• you can become overstimulated, jumpy and *panicky.* Your arms and legs may stiffen, and you might clench your jaw and grind your teeth – your face aches the next day
• you can start to **halluclina**te
• dancing for hours makes you too hot; you lose salt as you sweat and your **energy is sapped**. You become dehydrated, which can lead to heatstroke
• your memory may suddenly go. You become **unco-ordin**ated and **clumsy**
• as the effects wear off, you feel **life**less and your mood sinks
• you may feel **panicky, depressed and paranoid.**

ONTAIN RUBBISH, SUCH AS TALCUM POWDER

The real dangers

TEMPERATURE CONTROL Ecstasy interferes with the brain's thermostat, and your body temperature could rise well above normal. You may become *delirious* and start **hallucina**ting, and you could develop heatstroke, which can kill you.

BRAIN SWELLING Because you're so hot, you may drink too much water too quickly. This can cause the **brain to swell**, leading to unconsciousness and rapid death (within 12 hours).

WARNING! Ecstasy is particularly dangerous for anyone who has raised blood pressure or a heart condition.

Addictive?

Ecstasy is not addictive when used occasionally in small amounts. With heavy use the "loved-up" effects disappear and it becomes mainly a stimulant. Users who take ecstasy all weekend every weekend can suffer what resembles amphetamine dependence. They get withdrawal symptoms, such as exhaustion, sleeping for long periods during the day, insomnia at night, depression, paranoia and anxiety.

BAD TRIP The rush of brain chemicals can trigger nightmare **hallucina**tions. If you ever take ecstasy again, they can come back. You may feel you've got superhuman powers and overestimate your ability to do dangerous things, such as leaping from a great height.

BRAIN DAMAGE Ecstasy can **interrupt blood flow to the brain** and cause a stroke (yes, even in young people), resulting in paralysis, dementia (loss of memory and the ability to think clearly) and Parkinson's disease (when the body shakes and twitches uncontrollably).

LIVER AND KIDNEY FAILURE If you're susceptible, one pill can cause **fatal** kidney and liver failure and there's no way of predicting whether or not this is likely until it's too late.

LIFE-THREATENING CONDITION A **serious side effect**, sometimes called sledging, can come on if you mix ecstasy with any other drug. It can happen the first time you take a tablet if you're susceptible. You feel freezing cold and **shiver violently**, you feel like you're going to die – and you might. You can't talk or move. **You feel as though you're drifting into a sleep – from which you may never wake.**

The comedown

If you've had enough sleep, haven't smoked cannabis, haven't gone clubbing, danced all night or drunk alcohol, you stand a chance of feeling okay. However, your cheerful mood will have started to desert you on *Day 2*. By *Day 3* you'll be feeling **very low** and **irritable**. You won't be feeling any better on *Day 4*. Only on *Day 5* do you begin to recover your equilibrium.

• If you have been clubbing and haven't had enough sleep then this comedown will be worse.

• For some users, the low they experience after taking ecstasy is only relieved by repeating the cycle at the weekend, which means **they're continually under the influence of E** even if they only take it on Friday or Saturday night.

An ecstasy hangover is 10 times worse than an alcohol hangover

The Law

• *Ecstasy is a Class A drug,* **in the same category as heroin and cocaine.** *It's illegal to have, give away or sell.*

• *You can be done for dealing even if you have just two pills on you.*

• *You may receive a fine, a prison sentence or both, or you may be cautioned. It will depend upon your own personal circumstances, as well as on local police policies.*

Side effects of long-term use

Ecstasy drains the brain of a chemical called *serotonin* that regulates how happy you feel. So if you pop pills every weekend it can affect your mood, sleep and memory for up to two weeks, and you may risk suffering from **depression** in later life.

The ecstasy family

Ecstasy (MDMA) belongs to a "family" of man-made drugs and its "relatives" are sometimes passed off as E. But they're different and you might get a shock if you take them expecting the usual effect of MDMA.

• **MDA** (**m**ethylene**d**i**oxya**mphetamine), the parent drug, shares the amphetamine-like effects of ecstasy, but it's more **hall**u**c**i**no**geni**C** – more like acid – and lasts longer.

• **MDEA** (**m**ethylene**d**ioxy**e**thyl**a**mphetamine), sometimes known as EVE, is ecstasy's sister drug. It's like ecstasy in effect, except you don't get the same warm feelings about life and everyone around you – those are unique to true MDMA.

Precautions and warnings

Most recorded ecstasy deaths have happened because the tablet was not "pure" or because of a failure to counteract overheating correctly. It's tempting to drink too much water too quickly when trying to cool down, but it's better to **keep sipping water slowly over a long period of time**.

• Sip around a half-pint of liquid every half an hour. High-energy sports drinks are best, then fruit juice or water.

• **Keep salt levels up** by eating salted crisps or nuts.

• **Stay cool**: don't wear a hat, take off some clothes if you're hot and **take frequent rests** in the chill-out room.

• **NEVER take another tablet.** When the effect of one tablet is pleasant, the idea of taking another after a couple of hours may seem attractive but it's very dangerous. The body can't get rid of the ecstasy fast enough; the effects accelerate and are uncontrollable.

• **NEVER mix** ecstasy with any other drugs, including alcohol.

• Stay with friends and **know where to go for help.**

IF SOMETHING GOES WRONG ➡

panic attack

If your friend becomes paranoid, anxious and starts to panic take her to a quiet room. Offer her a hot drink or some water, and keep talking to her. Don't let her wander off. If your friend begins panting (hyperventilating), get her to breathe normally by copying you.

Overheating

Move your friend to a cool place and give him sips of high-energy sports drinks, fruit juice or water – don't let him drink too quickly. Splash cool water on his head if he's abnormally hot. Get medical help.

Bad trip

Your friend may see or hear frightening things that aren't really there – this is known as hallucinating. Reassure her that the things she can see or hear are imaginary and will soon pass. Stay with your friend until the bad trip is over.

Inability to speak or move

This may be the first sign of a life-threatening condition sometimes known as sledging. If your friend is also cold and begins to shiver violently, there is no time to lose. Keep your friend awake.

☎ **Call an ambulance**

unconsciousness

If your friend is breathing, place her in the recovery position (see page 120).

☎ **Call an ambulance**

Tell the medical staff what your friend has taken – it could save her life.

• Be prepared to resuscitate your friend if she stops breathing (see page 121).

• If your friend vomits while unconscious, check that she's still breathing.

If in doubt, phone the National Drugs Helpline 0800 77660

STIMULANTS ARE DANGEROUS FOR ANYONE WI

HERBAL HIGHS

What are herbal highs?

Herbal stimulants are increasingly popular, especially on the summer rock festival circuit. Herbal ecstasy, a blend of mildly psychoactive herbs or herb extracts, is openly sold as a "safe" alternative to ecstasy (MDMA). However, many types contain the drug ephedrine and can be extremely DANGEROUS.

WARNING! Ephedrine can be more dangerous than MDMA.

Herbal ecstasy

• Because it's a mild **stimulant**, energy, awareness and perception are likely to be increased, but how much and for how long depends on exactly what's in it. Some people claim that it has similar effects to ecstasy, but others have said that it's no more stimulating than a cup of coffee or a glass of cola.

• Herbal ecstasy that contains ephedrine can have **unpleasant side effects**, which may include jitteriness, tremors, headaches, insomnia, nausea and vomiting, fatigue, dizziness, chest pains and palpitations.

Street names
Herbal ecstasy, Herbal X-Tacy, Cloud 9

The Law
Herbal ecstasy is not a controlled substance.

form
Herbal ecstasy is usually sold in capsules.

Khat

Another herbal alternative is khat, a mild amphetamine-like **stimulant** derived from a leafy plant that grows in eastern Africa and the Arabian peninsula.

• Said to be like having a small dose of amphetamine; it makes the user *euphoric* and *talkative*. It can also have **calming** effects.

• Chewing khat causes inflammation of the mouth and infections, and overuse can cause cancer of the mouth.

• Prolonged and regular use of khat may cause **depression, anxiety and irritability**.

Street names
Khat, Qat, Quat

The Law
Khat is not a controlled substance in the UK.

form
Khat leaves are either chewed fresh or brewed into a tea. They're totally impure.

HEART CONDITION OR HIGH BLOOD PRESSURE

Street names

K, Special K, Vitamin K

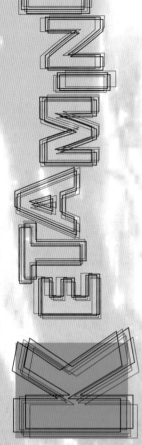

What is ketamine?

Ketamine is a "dissociative anaesthetic", which means it **detaches the mind from the body**. It's used as a **HORSE TRANQUILLIZER** and is related to the veterinary anaesthetic PCP, also known as angel dust.

form

On prescription ketamine comes as a clear liquid, but on the street it's a white powder or tablet. The powder is bought in a paper "wrap", similar to amphetamine, and can be swallowed or inhaled ("snorted"). The tablet is usually swallowed, but if ground up it can be inhaled.

The ketamine effect

• There's an initial rush, similar to the cocaine rush, that may happen within 30 seconds if the drug is injected, or 20–30 minutes if swallowed. Then it's **rapidly downhill for about the next three hours**.

• the body is numb and **p a r a l y s e d**

• there may be sickness and **vomiting**

• **co-ordina**ti**on go**es and the simplest tasks are impossible

• there's a feeling of being weightless and of being **sepa rated fr om t he bo dy**

• terrifying hallucinations can occur; limbs feel as though they're gr**owing** and **shrink**ing; there's tunnel vision and faces look grossly distorted. The **hallucina**tio**ns** seem as if they'll never stop and there's a feeling of being close to death.

The Law

• *Ketamine is not a controlled substance under the Misuse of Drugs Act so it's not illegal to possess it.*

• *Its sale and supply are controlled under the Medicines Act, so it's illegal to give it away or sell it.*

This is **HORRIBLE** stuff

• Ketamine is **not a dance drug** and taking it in a club is a bad idea. The noisy, disorientating environment will worsen the bad effects of ketamine.

• Never take it on the spur of the moment.

• **DON'T MIX KETAMINE** with any other drugs. Ketamine and speed, ketamine and acid, and ketamine and alcohol are all recipes for **disaster**.

Dangers

• It's easy to overdose – the potency varies so you never know how much you're taking.

• Ketamine damages your mind, so don't take it if you feel down or suffer from any kind of mental illness.

• Ketamine slows your heart-rate and breathing. The effect is exaggerated. If ketamine is mixed with depressants such as alcohol, heroin or tranquillizers, you could fall unconscious and die.

Ketamine and ecstasy

• Be aware. Ketamine is one of the drugs most often "cut" with MDMA in ecstasy pills.

• People sometimes say they've had a "smacky" E, meaning it made them feel s e d a t e d, instead of euphoric and energetic. In fact, this pill may have contained ketamine.

• Worse still, ketamine pills are sometimes sold as ecstasy so be careful. Ketamine has anything but the effect of an E, and can be **terrifying** for someone who isn't prepared for it.

IF SOMETHING GOES WRONG ➤

Bad trip

Your friend may see or hear frightening things that aren't really there – this is known as hallucinating. Reassure her that the things she can see or hear are imaginary and will soon pass. Stay with your friend until the bad trip is over.

unconsciousness

If your friend is breathing, place him in the recovery position (*see page 120*).

☎ **Call an ambulance.** Tell the medical staff what your friend has taken – it could save his life.

• Be prepared to resuscitate your friend if he stops breathing (*see page 121*).

• If your friend vomits while he's unconscious, check that he's still breathing.

If in doubt, phone the National Drugs Helpline 0800 776600

AY THEY DIDN'T ENJOY THE EXPERIENCE

Street names
GBH (Grievous Bodily Harm), Liquid Ecstasy, Liquid X

What is GHB?

GHB, which stands for *gamma**h**ydroxy**b**utyrate*, is an **anaesthetic** used to sedate patients before an operation. It's the drug that was implicated in the death of actor River Phoenix, and has, more recently, become popular in clubs, particularly on the gay scene. Like rohypnol, GHB is sometimes used to spike drinks.

form

• GHB is usually sold in bottles that contain about 40 ml of liquid.
• It may appear as a powder, tablet or capsule.
• It's swallowed and has a slightly salty taste.

An unknown quantity

This is very dangerous stuff because the concentration of the liquid varies from bottle to bottle. A bottle could contain 3 g, relatively little, or it could contain 20 g, a huge amount. It's virtually impossible to gauge the strength of the liquid so it's easy to overdose. The long-term effects of GHB aren't really known. **NEVER top up.**

WARNING! The difference between the effective amount and the lethal amount is very small.

The Law
GHB isn't controlled under the Misuse of Drugs Act in the UK so it's not illegal to have it. However, because it's classed as a medicine, it's illegal to sell it or give it away without proper authorization.

Don't mix with other drugs

The dangers will be increased if GHB is taken with other drugs, particularly depressants such as tranquillizers or alcohol.
Know the street names
If you swallow Liquid Gold (poppers) when you want Liquid X (GHB) you could end up in hospital. **Be careful.** Know what you're taking.

THE LONG-TERM EFFECTS OF GH

The GHB effect

The effect takes between 10 minutes and an hour to come on, depending on the amount that's taken, the concentration and the person's body weight.

• A small dose of GHB has a similar effect to alcohol. It lowers inhibitions and makes people more *sociable*, and even has a similar *euphoric* feeling to ecstasy.

• If the dose is high, the euphoria gives way to **powerful sedative effects,** making people feel **tired** and "doped out".

Grievous bodily harm

As the dosage is increased you may begin to suffer **the nastier side of GHB** – that's why it has the street name GBH. It's likely that you'll:

• feel sick and start to **vomit**
• get stiff and *p a i n f u l* muscles
• feel **dis**orientated
• have **fits** (convulsions)
• stop breathing and go into a **coma**.

WARNING!
Don't aid the research into GHB by becoming a statistic yourself.

Is it a sex drug?

It's claimed that GHB heightens sex drive, but this hasn't been proven. However, because of GHB's potential to lower inhibitions, users may become more sexually confident. In this event, everyone should make sure they're fully prepared to practise SAFE SEX.

IF SOMETHING GOES WRONG ➤

FITS

Ease your friend's fall if you can. Clear a space around her so that she can't hurt herself. Loosen clothing around her neck and put something soft under her head. When the fit stops, put her in the recovery position (*see page 120*).
☎ **Call an ambulance.**

unconsciousness

If your friend is breathing, place him in the recovery position (*see page 120*).
☎ **Call an ambulance.** Tell medical staff what your friend has taken – it could save his life.
• Be prepared to resuscitate your friend if he stops breathing (*see page 121*).

• If your friend vomits while unconscious, check that he's still breathing.

Some users of GHB who went into a coma have made a full recovery, but only because they received medical help quickly.

If in doubt, phone the National Drugs Helpline 0800 776600

ARE UNKNOWN AT THE MOMENT

What are solvents?

Most solvents are **volatile substances**, which means they give off a vapour and evaporate when in contact with air. The most common term associated with solvent abuse is "glue-sniffing", but glue is just one of many products that are "sniffed". A whole range of household items, such as aerosols, correcting fluid and nail polish, are abused.

WARNING!
Solvents kill more
people under 16
than any other
recreational
drug.

Street names
Glue, Gas, Huff,
Aerosols

All solvents are poisons

solvents

Solvents will rule your life

The solvent effect

The **hit** from solvents is strong, can be felt almost instantaneously and lasts about half an hour:

• people feel a sense of *euphoria*, and things seem very unreal. Users say it's like suddenly getting very **dr$_u$nk**

• the heart-rate and breathing shoot up, which makes people feel giddy and light-headed

• it's common to find it difficult to stand up or walk properly

• some users feel **happy, dreamy or excited,** and start giggling uncontrollably. Continuing to inhale beyond this point can lead to *unpleasant* **hallu$c$inations**

• also common is the feeling of invincibility. People have been known to leap out of windows or in front of speeding cars in the belief that they can survive anything.
THEY CAN'T.

form

Some of the most commonly abused and most dangerous substances are:

• liquid petroleum gases (butane and propane) found in many aerosols, fuel for camping stoves and lamps as well as in gas refills for cigarette lighters

• solvents (benzene and hexane) in nail polish and its remover, correcting fluid and dry-cleaning fluids

• solvent-based glues (toluene and hexane) often used for model building and D.I.Y.

SOLVENTS CAN CAUSE SUDDEN DEAT

Solvents usage

There are several ways in which solvents are abused and they all amount to inhaling the vapours they give off:

• they are poured on to a piece of cloth or into a plastic bag

(NEVER PUT A PLASTIC BAG OVER YOUR HEAD)

• most dangerous, is spraying the aerosol straight into the mouth which can freeze up the throat and the air passages so that breathing stops.

Someone doing this can die in a few minutes.

Are solvents addictive?

SOLVENTS If you stop using solvents, your body won't suffer withdrawal symptoms because they're not physically addictive. Solvents can, however, be **psychologically addictive**. Heavy or long-term **users feel they can't face life unless they're cloaked in a solvent haze.** Solvent abuse becomes their only escape from what they see as a dull or hopeless life.

TOLERANCE If you use solvents regularly, you'll build up a tolerance and need more to get the same effects, so there's an even greater risk of doing yourself harm.

COMING OFF SOLVENTS Withdrawal from solvents leads to powerful feelings of anxiety, depression and *nervousness*, but these effects will wear off.

GET HELP If you have a solvent abuse problem, phone the National Drugs Helpline on 0800 776600.

What some people do on solvents

You may be seriously disorientated and confused as if you're really drunk. In this state, anything could happen. Solvent abusers have been killed by:
• running into traffic
• falling into a canal or river and drowning
• accidentally starting a fire
• literally "exercising to death".
The adrenaline stimulated by solvent sniffing can make you hyperactive and cause you to overexert yourself, for example, by running for a long time or lifting something very heavy. And as your heart will already be working overtime, the extra strain could cause a heart attack. All these dangers are increased if you're hallucinating. You may be running away from a frightening vision or think you're able to do the impossible, such as stop traffic.
This isn't a joke: these things have happened.

The Law

It's not illegal to possess or misuse solvents. It is, however, a criminal offence to supply (sell or give) a solvent for inhalation to a person who is under the age of 18.

• If the police see a group of you sniffing a solvent, they'll probably ask you to move along or detain you so that they can make enquiries about your welfare.

• If your behaviour is at all threatening or aggressive after you've been using solvents, the police may arrest you.

WARNING! All solvents are highly inflammable – and the vapour they give off (which you can't see) can be explosive.

Effects to make you think twice

Death or serious injury can result from solvent abuse.

• You may overexert yourself or have an accident, and some ways of using solvents can lead to suffocation and death in minutes.

• The poisons, or toxins, in solvents also pose a real threat. **Many of the chemicals attack body organs**, particularly the liver and heart, leading to disease, organ failure and even death.

• Solvents also cause your body to produce a lot of adrenaline, which gives you a burst of energy that increases your heart-rate dramatically. This sudden change may make you very sick and if you're sick while unconscious, you may choke to death, or it can put such a strain on your heart, that it stops suddenly and you may die.

Safety first

Inhaling solvents is exceedingly dangerous so stay away from them if you can. However, if you do inhale solvents lower the risks:

• never spray an aerosol or lighter refill directly into your mouth

• never put a bag of solvent over your head

• stay in a group: if something goes wrong, a friend can get help or calm you down

• never use solvents frequently – **even once a week is too often**

• avoid busy roads, rivers, railways and the tops of buildings so, if you hallucinate, you're less likely to injure yourself

• don't overexert yourself: it's a bad idea to do any strenuous exercise after sniffing.

FIVE TIMES MORE PEOPLE DIE FROM SOLVENTS TH

Effects not to be sniffed at

There are other effects of solvent abuse that won't kill you, but won't thrill you either. Repeated use can lead to lots of physical and psychological side effects.

SKIN RASHES The skin around your mouth and nose becomes irritated.

HANGOVER It's common to become **tired** and have a thick head.

"At first sniffing was excellent. I thought, 'How dangerous can the stuff be if Mum gets it at the supermarket?' Then one of us collapsed. I saw him in hospital just a body full of tubes. That was it – I haven't done it since."

WEIGHT LOSS AND SHAKES You look **terrible** and feel even worse.

LIVER AND KIDNEY FAILURE The toxins **poison** these vital organs. If they fail you'll die.

SHORT-TERM MEMORY LOSS **You become forgetful and can't concentrate on anything.**

MOOD SWINGS You'll be smiling one minute and aggressive the next.

DEPRESSION The only way to beat the depression is to kick the habit.

If you stop using solvents, any side effects will clear up. It's not a lost cause and you can get back to normal, so give it up.

IF SOMETHING GOES WRONG

Bad trip
Your friend may begin to see or hear frightening things that aren't really there – this is known as hallucinating and may cause your friend to panic. Reassure her that the things she can see or hear are imaginary and will soon pass. Stay with your friend.

Burns
If your friend has serious burns, call an ambulance immediately. Meanwhile, try to cool the affected area with cold water and make your friend as comfortable as possible.

unconsciousness
If your friend is breathing, place him in the recovery position (*see page 120*).
☎ **Call an ambulance.** Tell the medical staff what your friend has taken – it could save his life.
• Be prepared to resuscitate your friend if he stops breathing (*see page 121*).
• If your friend vomits while unconscious, check that he's still breathing.

Important
Get the solvent away from your friend immediately. Open any doors and windows.

If in doubt, phone the National Drugs Helpline 0800 776600

OM ECSTASY, AMPHETAMINE AND COCAINE COMBINED

What are poppers?

This is a group of quick-acting drugs (alkyl nitrites), of which amyl nitrite, butyl nitrite and isobutyl nitrite are the most widely available. Poppers evaporate at room temperature and are inhaled. They're **stimulants** but the "rush" lasts minutes, hence the name "poppers".

WARNING!
Don't drink poppers. They're highly toxic and this will result in unconsciousness and very possibly death.

POPPERS

form

• Small bottles, or occasionally glass vials, of clear gold-coloured liquid that's inhaled from the bottle or from a cloth soaked in it.
• Fresh poppers smell sweet and fruity, but the stale chemical smells like old socks.

Know the street names

Drugs have many different street names and some of them sound similar. If you tried to sniff Liquid X (GHB) instead of Liquid Gold (poppers) not much would happen. But if you swallowed poppers when you wanted GHB, it could be fatal.

Street names   **Amyl, Rush, Rave, Stage, Liquid Gold, Stud, Ram**

The poppers effect

The effects from inhaling poppers are instantaneous, but very short lived. There may be:
• a burst of **energy**, and a rushing sensation, because the heart starts beating faster
• a feeling of light-headedness after the initial rush because blood pressure is reduced. This can lead to dizziness, loss of balance and even fainting
• a sense that time has slowed down
• a lowering of sexual inhibition, and possibly a feeling of being *sexually aroused*.

Why you won't like it

• Fainting is never a good move. You'll not only feel foolish coming round, but you may also injure yourself when you fall.
• You may also feel very sick and have a ThumPing heaDache – if you're in a club, you probably won't feel like dancing.

The risks

You may be able to find poppers in a joke shop, but they're no joke. They're not addictive, but the effects can be pretty unpleasant. Apart from fainting, nausea and headaches, users can suffer other problems.

• Because alkyl nitrites *SPEED UP* heart-rate and **lower** blood pressure they're dangerous for anyone with a heart or blood-pressure condition.

• Regular use can lead to skin problems around the nose and mouth.

• Nitrites are caustic, which means they'll burn skin if spilt.

• Inhaling vapours increases the pressure on your eyeball so is very dangerous if you suffer from an eye condition, such as glaucoma.

• Increased sexual arousal and decreased sexual inhibitions are a dangerous combination – you're more likely to have casual sex, so be aware of the risks of contracting HIV/AIDS and other sexually transmitted diseases.

BE SENSIBLE

• **DON'T** keep taking more hits – you'll just feel worse and increase your chances of nasty effects with every hit.

• **DON'T** use poppers with other drugs – you're just creating bad effects.

• **DON'T** mix poppers with alcohol – you're even more likely to collapse or have a potentially disastrous sexual encounter.

The Law

Alkyl nitrites are not covered by the Misuse of Drugs Act. However, amyl nitrite is a controlled medicine, which means possession without a prescription is illegal, as is supply.

IF SOMETHING GOES WRONG ➡

Burns

If nitrites burn your skin, run cold water over the area for about 20 minutes.

Poisoning

If your friend has swallowed poppers, ☎ **call an ambulance**. If she's conscious, give her frequent sips of cold water or milk. Don't try to make her sick.

FAINTING

If your friend feels faint, take him somewhere quiet and lay him down with his feet in the air. Give him some cola to drink (nothing else is as good). Don't let him stand up too quickly.

unconsciousness

If your friend is breathing, place her in the recovery position (*see page 120*). ☎ **Call an ambulance**. Tell the medical staff what your friend has taken – it could save her life.

• Be prepared to resuscitate your friend if she stops breathing (*see page 121*).

• If your friend vomits while unconscious, check that she's still breathing.

If in doubt, phone the National Drugs Helpline 0800 776600

AND KNOW WHAT YOU'RE TAKING

Street names
**Speed, Whizz,
Sulphates, Billy,
Uppers**

What is amphetamine?

Amphetamine is short for
Alpha**M**ethyl**PHE**ne**T**hyl**AMINE**, a man
made drug first created over 100 years
ago. It's a powerful **stimulant** that triggers
the central nervous system, making a
person more **alert** and **energetic**.

form

• Amphetamine comes
as a white powder that
looks like salt, or
sometimes as a pill or
paste.
• The powder usually
comes in a folded
paper envelope called
a "wrap" that contains
about 1 g of powder.
• However, most wraps
only contain about
5 mg of actual
amphetamine as it's
often been "cut" with
rubbish to pad it out.
The extras could harm
you, especially if
snorted or injected.
No-one knows how
much is in a wrap –
even half a wrap can
have a powerful effect.

Amphetamine usage

SWALLOWING Amphetamine is **least
dangerous** when swallowed.
INHALING Some users sniff ("snort") speed
up the nose, through a straw or a rolled-up
banknote, which produces a faster, *more
intense* effect than swallowing it.
Snorting is, however, rough on the nostrils
(one user described it as "like shoving chilli
powder up your nose").
INJECTING Some users inject speed, which
is **extremely dangerous**. There's a real
chance of overdosing because you never
know how strong the dosage is, and the
heart can't take the shock. What's more, if
you share needles, you risk being infected
with HIV/AIDS and hepatitis B and C.
So don't inject.

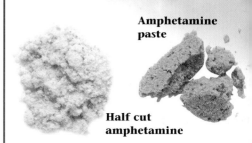

**Amphetamine
paste**

**Half cut
amphetamine**

THE HIGHS GET LESS HIGH AND THE LOW

How does it work?

Amphetamine **stimulates** the nervous system. It acts like adrenaline: your blood pressure goes up, your heart thumps and your body temperature rises.

The amphetamine effect

The effects of amphetamine are quite predictable, but only when a very small amount is taken. More can cause unexpected adverse reactions.

• Within 20–30 minutes of swallowing speed (less if it's snorted or injected) there's a "rush" through the body and a feeling of being **energetic, alert and self-confident.**

• **Everything s p e e d s up** and seems urgent. Users feel they're capable of doing things beyond their ability, such as driving safely at a high speed. **THEY AREN'T.**

• There's often a sense of feeling pumped up that lasts for hours. People stay awake for long periods and dance non-stop.

• People become very **talkative** but, although what they say will sound good to them, it's likely to be gibberish. They may start talking to strangers, which isn't a good idea.

• Amphetamine raises body temperature, so there's **a real risk of overheating**, which can be very dangerous especially if it's taken with alcohol or ecstasy.

Brief history

Amphetamines were discovered in 1887 by a German chemist. In the 1930s they became popular as over-the-counter "pep pills". Soldiers were given amphetamines during the Second World War to stop them from falling asleep on the job. In the 1960s, people began to take them so that they could party all night. In the 1970s, amphetamine sulphate became an illegal recreational drug.

Is it addictive?

Strictly speaking, speed isn't addictive. Users don't become dependent quickly, BUT with regular use they will reach a stage where they can't manage without it. The only way to combat the depression and exhaustion that can follow a speed high is to take more. And if this goes on for days, you'll finally collapse, becoming jittery and paranoid as if suffering from a psychotic illness.

ET MUCH LOWER WITH PROLONGED USE

Looking after number one

STAY WITH FRIENDS Being with friends may improve your mood, and you'll be able to look out for each other. Make sure you tell each other what you've taken.

REPLACE LOST FLUIDS Sip a half-pint of liquid every half an hour: high-energy sports drinks are best, then fruit juice or water. **Don't drink alcohol** – it makes you more dehydrated, and is nasty when combined with amphetamine.

REPLACE LOST SALTS When you sweat, your body loses a lot of salt and minerals. To replace these, and avoid aching limbs the next morning, eat salted crisps or peanuts. This isn't easy as you won't feel hungry.

COOL DOWN REGULARLY Non-stop dancing can cause overheating. **The chill-out room is there to help your body to recover, so use it**. You can also splash water on your face, or try going outside. Don't wear a hat – you're more likely to overheat.

Drinking enough

Taking stimulants in a hot club raises your body temperature even more. If you're dancing for hours your temperature is likely to go through the roof. If you OVERHEAT your body sweats buckets and **you must replace these lost fluids***. Make sure you drink a half-pint of non-alcoholic liquid every half an hour. BUT DON'T DRINK TOO MUCH WATER TOO QUICKLY.*

Speed and ecstasy

Many people combine amphetamine and ecstasy because they want the good feeling of ecstasy and the energy of amphetamine. But this double combination of stimulants means that you're twice as likely to get heatstroke or have a heart attack.

It's not always a bed of roses

Taking amphetamine doesn't necessarily lead to a fun-filled evening. Different people react in different ways:

• the rush of energy you feel may make you **anxious** and nervy, instead of self-confident – you may even have a *panic attack*

• your pounding heart and twitching limbs may make you feel out of control and one step away from a heart attack

• you can still be "wired" 12 hours after taking even a small amount, and unable to sleep. For the next few days you'll feel **run down** and **low.** In addition, you'll have wrecked your body's sleeping pattern

• you may also need to go to the toilet a lot.

BE CAREFUL: THE DANCE/DRUG COMBINATIO

Not looking after number one

There can be some serious physical side effects to taking amphetamine.

OVERHEATING A rocketing body temperature over 38°C will make you **delirious**. If you're dehydrated, you risk getting **heatstroke**, which can result in unconsciousness.

BRAIN SWELLING If you drink too much water too quickly your brain may suffer **water poisoning**, leading to unconsciousness and rapid death. The risk depends on how much you sweat, but drinking more than three pints of water per hour is **very dangerous**.

PAIN AND SICKNESS You may get body cramps, a splitting headache and be *SICK*.

INCREASED HEART-RATE Even if you're young and healthy, using amphetamine can lead to a **heart attack**. Your heart could stop altogether and that equals DEATH.

LIVER AND KIDNEY FAILURE Can occur if a high dose of speed is mixed with alcohol, and both conditions are **fatal**.

HIGH BLOOD PRESSURE Small blood vessels may burst in your brain, leading to paralysis or coma.

HYPERVENTILATION Your breathing may be irregular.

LIFE-THREATENING CONDITION An extreme reaction, sometimes called sledging, to mixing amphetamine with other drugs, such as ecstasy, ketamine or alcohol. It could happen the first time you take it. You'll be freezing cold and shivering violently; **you'll feel like you're going to die** (and you might); you'll be unable to speak or move your body; you'll feel as though you're drifting into a sleep from which you won't wake (and you might not).

IF YOU SEE SOMEONE WITH ANY OF THESE SYMPTOMS, ☎ **call an ambulance IMMEDIATELY**.

Speed and alcohol

Drinking alcohol increases the adverse effects of speed. It also makes you less inhibited and more likely to become aggressive and/or sexually aroused. The combination gives you the confidence and energy to persist with sexual advances or violent urges, and makes you more likely to drink more alcohol. This may result in you fighting, or having casual sex with all the usual risks that brings, such as sexually transmitted diseases or unwanted pregnancy.

WARNING!
The effects of amphetamine can be even more dangerous for someone who has a heart condition or high blood pressure.

AN CAUSE REAL PROBLEMS

The Law

• *Amphetamine is a Class B drug –* **this doesn't mean it's safer than Class A drugs.**

• *You may be charged with possession if you have a small amount of amphetamine on you. However, the more you have the less likely it is to be for your own use and you may be charged with possession with intent to supply.*

• *The penalty for possession with intent to supply is jail and/or a large fine.*

What goes up must come down

This is the bit no-one tells you about. As the high wears off:

• all your energy will drain out of you
• you'll become lethargic, weak and *tired*
• you may feel slightly paranoid and depressed
• you may well worry about trivial things
• you may well feel **isolated** and out of touch with people around you
• you'll feel utterly exhausted but your brain will still be racing and sleep will be impossible.

DON'T TAKE TRANQUILLIZERS

Some people take tranquillizers to help them sleep. You just don't know how your body is going to react to this sort of drug cocktail, either short- or long-term. SO DON'T TAKE THE RISK.

WARNING! Don't take more drugs to "cheat" the comedown: this only delays the inevitable and the comedown will be much worse when it finally happens.

Handling the comedown

• Go home or to a friend's house with a group of people with whom you're comfortable.
• To relax and warm up, have a shower, put on clean clothes and make some sweet tea. It's easy to catch cold after clubbing, especially if you're wearing a T-shirt drenched in sweat.
• You won't feel like it, but eat and drink well. High-energy sports drinks, chocolate, milk shakes, fruit juice, bananas, cereal and ice cream are all good.
• Put on some soothing music; avoid music with a rhythmic beat – your heart will start pounding again and it'll make you panicky.
• Try to get some sleep. It's the only way you'll be able to recover.

Both mind and body need help during a comedown

The price your body pays

It's your body as well as your pocket that pays. Your body has been forced by the amphetamine to provide extra energy, and this energy "loan" has to be paid back when the drug wears off. You'll be exhausted and feel **terrible.** Heavy, regular amphetamine use can also have serious psychological effects: it can lead to a complete mental breakdown and amphetamine psychosis, which means **you become paranoid, agitated and suspicious of everybody.**

> **WARNING!**
> Never let yourself get to the stage where you feel you HAVE to use stimulants. If you do use them, only do it occasionally: give your mind and body a break.

IF SOMETHING GOES WRONG

panic attack

If your friend is paranoid, anxious and starts to panic take her to a quiet room away from large groups of people and try to reassure her. Offer her a hot drink or some water, and keep talking to her. Don't let her wander off alone. If your friend begins panting (hyperventilating), get her to try to breathe normally by copying you.

unconsciousness

If your friend is breathing, place him in the recovery position (*see page 120*).

☎ **Call an ambulance.** Tell the medical staff what your friend has taken – it could save his life.

• Be prepared to resuscitate your friend if he stops breathing (*see page 121*).

• If your friend vomits while unconscious, check that he's still breathing.

Overheating

Move your friend to a cool place and give her sips of high-energy sports drinks, fruit juice or water – don't let her drink too quickly as this is very dangerous.
Splash cool water on her head if she's abnormally hot. Get medical help.

Inability to speak or move

This may be the first sign of a life-threatening condition sometimes known as sledging. If your friend is also cold and begins to shiver violently, there is no time to lose. Keep your friend awake.

☎ **Call an ambulance.**

If in doubt, phone the National Drugs Helpline 0800 776600

S THEIR COMEDOWN TAKES MUCH LONGER

Street names **Ice, Crystal, Meth, Ice cream, Glass**

What is methylamphetamine?

Methylamphetamine or methamphetamine is a man-made **stimulant**. It's like amphetamine but MUCH stronger. It's to amphetamine what crack is to cocaine – it can be 90–100 per cent pure.

form

• Creamy white or sandy-coloured powder sold in wraps like amphetamine.
• Tablets in different shapes, colours and sizes. Some have names such as "speed king" stamped on them.
• Clear and colourless crystals, like glass, sold in bags. Large crystals (bombs) are bought individually wrapped in plastic film or cigarette papers.

Methylamphetamine usage

Swallowing The least dangerous method and it takes about half an hour to take effect. Far smaller amounts are used than with amphetamine for the drug to take effect.
Smoking Users get an *intense* and almost immediate **hit** from inhaling the vapours given off by heating crystals. The powder is not usually smoked because the heating process breaks it down, lessening the effect.
NEVER INJECT METHYLAMPHETAMINE, AND NEVER MIX IT WITH OTHER DRUGS.

The methylamphetamine effect

A minute amount of this *nasty stimulant* gives an incredible hit – **it's that powerful**. The feelings are not short lived; one hit can last for hours, depending on the user's tolerance and the amount taken.
• The "rush" is very intense with sensations of *euphoria*, **energy** and **invincibility** that can be almost overwhelming.
• Some users feel *sexually aroused.*

METHYLAMPHETAMINE IS ONE OF THE MOS

What you might not like

Methylamphetamine can trigger unpleasant hallucinations that make you lose control of your actions and emotions. People have assaulted and even raped under the influence of methylamphetamine.

A very big comedown

The comedown is a real kick in the teeth – it's far worse than coming down from amphetamine:

• you can feel *exhausted* and **achy** for days
• you feel d e p r e s s e d , **nervous and panicky**
• after a few weeks of use your behaviour becomes bizarre, you're paranoid, you suffer delusions, even psychosis. Methylamphetamine can even trigger **schizophrenia**.

Slipping and sliding on ice

This is a really *NASTY* drug – side effects may kill.
• There's a risk of a stroke or a heart attack. It also raises your body temperature, which can lead to heatstroke especially if you're in a club and taking other drugs – **heatstroke can kill**.
• Tolerance builds up quickly with continuous use. Eventually, you may need dangerous amounts to get near the original effect.
• **There's a real risk of overdose** and even a tiny amount could be too much for your body – it can happen the first time it's taken. If you overdose you may suffer convulsions, which can lead to unconsciousness and even death.

It's addictive

• Within a short time **physical dependence**, similar to dependence on crack, could develop.
• If you use this drug regularly, you'll become so **psychologically dependent** that you can't face the world without it.
• Withdrawal can lead to depression, *panic attacks* and paranoia.

The Law

• *Methylamphetamine is a Class B drug so it's illegal to have, give away or sell.*
• *If prepared for injection, it becomes a Class A drug,* **with penalties on the same level as cocaine or heroin**.

Getting help

If you or anyone you know has a problem with methylamphetamine, get professional help.

■ ■ *IF SOMETHING GOES WRONG* ■ ➡

See pages 120–23.

If in doubt, phone the National Drugs Helpline 0800 776600

➡**WERFUL AND MOST DANGEROUS DRUGS**

How it works

When "snorted", cocaine is absorbed through the blood vessels in the nostrils, and reaches the brain in seconds. It stimulates the nervous system, increasing the heart-rate, and raising body temperature and blood pressure.

Brief history

German scientists isolated the drug cocaine from the coca leaf in the mid-19th century. When Coca Cola was introduced in 1886, the average glass contained a few milligrams of cocaine, until it was replaced by caffeine in 1903. Cocaine was touted as an over-the-counter tonic throughout Europe and America, until its addictive properties became obvious. It was declared illegal in America in 1914.

What is cocaine?

The cocaine found on the streets is a substance called *cocaine hydrochloride*. It's made by refining the leaves of the coca bush, which grows mainly in Bolivia, Colombia and Peru. Cocaine is a powerful **stimulant** that has similar properties to amphetamine. It was used for medicinal purposes as an over-the-counter "tonic" until it was found to be a **dangerous drug**; many of the people who'd taken it had become addicts.

WARNING! Cocaine is highly addictive.

Street cocaine is never pure

form

Most street cocaine comes as a white crystalline powder that looks like very fine salt. It's usually bought in a "wrap" containing 1 g of powder, although no-one can know how much of that gram is actually cocaine. When the coca plant is processed, the cocaine powder is about 85 per cent pure, but by the time it's sold on the street it's nowhere near this level. As the batch passes from dealer to dealer, it's "cut" or watered down with sugars, such as glucose and lactose, or even anaesthetics. Although cocaine has been found in concentrations as high as 60 per cent, on the streets it's often as low as 30 per cent cocaine – the rest is rubbish.

The cocaine effect

Felt in seconds, the effects rarely last more than half an hour. The strength depends on the potency of the cocaine, the setting in which it's taken, how often it's taken and the user's tolerance level.

• There's a sense of *euphoria* and *well-being*.

• Life looks rosy; stress and anxiety fall away.

• **Energy levels rise** and people want to be active, chat, laugh and **dance**.

• Everything said seems spot on: opinions, however outrageous, are just right and jokes seem incredibly funny, even when they're not.

• **Inhibitions go** and some people feel sexually *aroused*.

The cocaine low

The payback for an instant, intense high is a sudden, **deep low.** It comes on fast and hits hard. You'll be tempted to beat this low by taking more cocaine. This will take you back up, but it won't be as intense and it won't last long. The next low, on the other hand, will be even deeper.

• Even though the euphoria and confidence will have worn off, your brain will still be racing. You'll be unable to sleep and probably just become depressed, and even **PA RA NOID.**

• You'll get to sleep eventually, but when you wake you'll feel *tired* and *irritable*. Just as the night before everything seemed to go your way, it now feels as if the whole world is against you.

• You may start to feel *panicky* and threatened. If you've taken a large amount **you could start acting strangely and violently.**

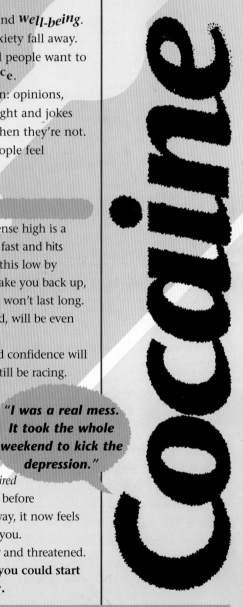

Street names
Coke, Charlie, Toot, Chang, Snow, Bolivian Marching Powder, White Lady

"I was a real mess. It took the whole weekend to kick the depression."

IT'S A FINE LINE WITH COCAINE

The Law

Cocaine is a Class A drug and carries the highest penalties for possession, use and supply.

- *Simply being in possession of cocaine could mean a prison sentence and an unlimited fine.*
- *Intent to supply or supplying cocaine could even lead to life imprisonment as well as a fine.*

Cocaine usage

- Most users divide the cocaine into "lines" with a razor blade or credit card. Then they sniff it up one nostril through a small tube, or through a rolled-up card or bank note.
- Less dangerous than sniffing is to eat cocaine in small amounts mixed with food or drink; it will have an effect – it just takes longer.
- Some people rub cocaine on their gums. Because cocaine is also a natural anaesthetic, this causes the gums to go numb.

NEVER INJECT

A few users inject cocaine to get a *faster* and more **intense** hit but that's very dangerous. There's a risk of infection from shared needles and a real possibility of overdosing. If you overdose, the heart-rate speeds up to a dangerous level and the body can't cope. This leads to unconsciousness and rapid death.

Don't mix with other drugs

Mixing cocaine with other drugs, including alcohol, is **extremely dangerous** Although you may get away with it a few times, you won't get away with it forever. If you get overconfident with cocaine, you'll regret it.

A speedball can kill

Speeding to disaster

When cocaine is mixed with heroin and injected it's called a speedball. This is a really bad idea because the two drugs worsen each other's effects. The heroin hides the unpleasant edginess of cocaine and lulls you into taking another dose of cocaine or heroin or both, **increasing your chances of a lethal overdose.**

Don't come down with downers

Some people take tranquillizers to get to sleep after a cocaine session – don't. Any mixture of depressants and stimulants is dangerous.

IF YOU KEEP TAKING MORE, THE HI

Addiction: the snowball effect

Anyone thinking about taking cocaine needs to know the whole deal. Although physical addiction is rare, **psychological dependence is a real possibility**. As the good feeling wears off the bad feelings swamp you so you soon feel that you want to take more. Although another hit takes you **back up**, it only puts off the inevitable **comedown** and when it does eventually happen the crash is even worse. You'll then be tempted to take yet another dose and so on. You're now well on the way to psychological addiction and once you're on that road, **it's very difficult to get off**. With regular cocaine use psychological dependence can become extremely deep-rooted and difficult to treat.

Cocaine leads to harder drugs

Cocaine rules your life

If you become an addict, you'll spend a lot of money supporting your habit. You'll become moody, unpredictable and generally unpleasant to be around. You'll be unable to do school work. On top of that, feeding such an expensive habit often leads to **a life of crime**.

Keep using and losing

Long-term cocaine use leads to terrible side effects.

Extreme paranoia

You'll become depressed and PA RA NOID and may even show symptoms of a severe mental illness called cocaine psychosis.

Weight loss

You'll become alarmingly underweight and malnourished.

Impotence

Male users won't be able to get or maintain an erection.

Chronic insomnia

Sleep becomes a thing of the past. You'll be exhausted but you won't be able to sleep; the simplest tasks will be beyond you.

Nasal nasties

"Snorting" burns a hole between your nostrils.

WARNING! Anyone with raised blood pressure or a heart condition should stay well away from cocaine.

ILL JUST GET LESS INTENSE

Kicking cocaine

Some people manage to only use cocaine occasionally; but if you're **vulnerable** in any way (shy, lacking confidence, low self-esteem) you risk quickly becoming dependent. Once addiction has set in, withdrawal symptoms include **anxiety, depression, panic attacks and paranoia**. These can be extremely hard to overcome and often lead to users craving more cocaine. For some, suicide seems the only way out – sadly, many such suicides have been recorded.

To kick cocaine, get professional help: phone the National Drugs Helpline on 0800 776600.

Out of control

You'll think you're in control of cocaine, until you wake up one day and find it has you by the throat – by then it could already be too late.

WARNING! Cocaine won't make your problems go away, it will just add to them so stay away from it.

Cocaine withdrawal is extremely tough

IF SOMETHING GOES WRONG

panic attack

If your friend is paranoid, anxious and starts to panic, take her to a quiet room away from large groups of people and try to reassure her. Offer her a hot drink or some water, and keep talking to her. Don't let her wander off alone. If your friend begins panting (hyperventilating), get her to try to breathe normally by copying your breathing.

unconsciousness

If your friend is breathing, place him in the recovery position (*see page 120*).
☎ **Call an ambulance.** Tell the medical staff what your friend has taken – it could save his life.

• Be prepared to resuscitate your friend he stops breathing (*see page 121*).

• If your friend is sick while unconscious che that he's still breathing

If in doubt, phone the National Drugs Helpline 0800 77660C

IF YOU INJECT COCAINE OR CRAC

What is crack?

Crack is cocaine that has been processed ("washed up") and it can be 80–100 per cent pure cocaine – much higher and therefore more **dangerous** than the 30–60 per cent purity of street cocaine. Crack vaporizes more quickly and enters the body faster than cocaine. It affects the body in the same way as cocaine, but to a far greater extent. Freebase is another rarer form of processed cocaine.

form

CRACK comes as crystals that look like small rocks. Some of the "pieces" look like grains of sand, although normally they're as much as 2 cm across. They vary in colour from pale yellow or pink, to white. FREEBASE is a fine white powder that looks a bit like icing sugar.

Street names
Rock, Wash, Stone, Roxanne, Cloud, Flake, Nuggets, Nine
Street names for freebase
Base, Baseball

The crack effect

Crack is generally smoked. According to users the intensity of the hit can't be exaggerated; it comes within seconds, but it's short lived. For a few minutes, 15 at the most, crack gives:
• an intense euphoria and elation, and a great **surge of energy**
• an incredible sense of *well-being* and power. Of all the drugs on the street, crack packs the **biggest** punch.

WARNING!
Crack is the strongest and nastiest stimulant of them all.

MAY BE TOO LATE FOR REGRETS

N E V E R   I N J E C T   C R A C K

Just don't inject. Injecting doesn't give a bigger hit, and there's a real danger of overdosing or becoming infected with HIV/AIDS and hepatitis B and C from shared needles and any other equipment used (the works).

What happens next?

Crack may take you straight up but in as little as five minutes, and rarely more than 15, the rush starts to wear off. Within 20 minutes of a crack hit the comedown begins:

• you've got the shakes and are **twitching** uncontrollably
• you're **shivering** as if you were in a deep-freeze
• you're weak and tired
• you're paranoid and **depressed**
• you feel alone and threatened by those around you
• you're **irritable** and **AGGRESSIVE**.
And this comedown can last for days.

How low can you go?

• Crack users say you can't begin to describe how awful the low is. **It's not so much like jumping off a cliff as tumbling down a slope covered in broken glass.**
• Regular users feel the need to keep taking larger and larger amounts of crack to get even near the original hit.

Crack bender

Users have been known to smoke large amounts of crack every day for several weeks. Taking so much crack always leads to indescribable withdrawal symptoms, a hellish comedown and a real risk of death.

On the rocks – crack's other nasty surprises

Long-term crack use – and that means weeks not years – can lead to lots of other problems.

Psychological problems

You feel intense aggression, hatred and distrust of other people, even friends and family. You become psychotic, delusional and violent, lose all contact with reality and are unable to judge any situation properly.

Social problems

Many users sell everything they own to fund their habit. Crack is expensive – £200 a day is nothing out of the ordinary. When there's nothing left to sell, crime may be the only option and a prison sentence the most likely outcome.

Complete isolation

When you're coming down you won't want to be with anyone and they won't want you. The isolation gets worse; life isn't worth living.

IT'S EASY TO LOSE CONTROL C

Crack IS addictive

Crack has been labelled the "one hit and you're hooked" drug. This isn't strictly true, but the nature of the drug is such that if you try it, **your chances of becoming addicted are higher than with ANY other drug.** Your physical addiction is very powerful because crack gives you an **intense high** followed almost immediately by a **terrible low** – your body's response is to crave more. You can also become psychologically dependent and feel you can't face the world without the drug. But what you don't realize is that it's the crack that's making your life so unbearable.

If you have a problem with crack, **you MUST get professional help.**

"Before you know it, crack takes over your mind. You're obsessed by it. You'll do anything for it."

Kicking crack

It's extremely tough to kick crack because the craving is so strong. If you use it on anything near a regular basis, or go on a crack binge, then you will suffer severe and horrible withdrawal symptoms which also make you want more.

You become **disorientated, panicky, depressed and paranoid**. This often leads to users becoming **suicidal**.

Drug combinations

Crack is so powerful in its own right that using any drug alongside it is potentially lethal. **Some users take heroin to ease the comedown. It's that bad.**

The Law

• *Crack is a Class A drug. It's illegal to have, sell or give to your friends and carries the highest level of penalties.*

• *The penalty for possessing crack for your own use is a long prison sentence and an unlimited fine.*

• *Possession with intent to supply (and there's no minimum amount) can lead to life imprisonment and an unlimited fine.*

IF SOMETHING GOES WRONG ➡

See pages 120–23.

If in doubt, phone the National Drugs Helpline 0800 776600

RACK. IT'S THE BOSS, NOT YOU

HEROIN

Heroin (*diamorphine hydrochloride*) is produced by processing raw opium, a natural substance found in oriental opium poppies. It's a **depressant drug** so its properties are basically the opposite of a stimulant drug, such as amphetamine. Because heroin is a "narcotic analgesic", it numbs the brain and body and kills pain.

WARNING!
Brown can sometimes be dissolved in vinegar or lemon juice, but both contain a fungus that can cause sight problems if injected.

form

Heroin comes in three forms: brown, china white and pharmaceutical heroin.

Brown
• The most common form, this is in fact diamorphine base – the hydrochloride bit has been removed.
• It's a brown powder, although the colour can vary from creamy white to dark coffee. The lighter the colour, the higher the heroin content.
• Brown is low-grade, messy, dirty stuff. The heroin content varies from 10 to 60 per cent. The rest is rubbish, "cut" with the heroin to bulk out the quantity.
• Brown is smoked – it should never be injected.

China white
• Found as grey granules that look a little like instant coffee.
• Although china white is smoked, it can also be injected.

Pharmaceutical heroin
• Pure heroin for medical use, it comes as a pure white powder or tablets, or as ampoules of clear liquid.

Street names
H, Smack, Junk, Horse, Harry, Brown, Gravy

How heroin works

As a **depressant drug**, heroin dulls the central nervous system:
- the heart beats more slowly
- breathing slows down and becomes shallower, so less oxygen is taken in
- blood pressure falls.

WARNING! Pharmaceutical heroin is so powerful that users of brown can overdose and die if they switch.

The heroin effect

The heroin effect is **BIG** – bigger than almost any other drug. It's a really powerful feeling that has no comparison in normal life. When heroin is injected intravenously, the "**hit**" is almost instantaneous, but even when it's smoked it only takes a few seconds.

- Feelings of *euphoria* and **waves of incredible well-being** flood in. All **pain** – physical and mental – **disappears**.
- **The addictive effect** is that you really love yourself.
- In small quantities heroin makes people very **talkative, energized, impassioned and confident**.
- Larger quantities send people into a trance-like state – they lose themselves in an interior world and they can't and don't want to communicate with anyone.
- The initial "*rush*" is **followed by a mellow, chilled-out feeling** that makes the world look rosy.
- The heroin effect **starts to wear off after 1–2 hours**, depending on tolerance levels and how often it's used. It will have worn off completely after anything from 3–6 hours.

Brief history

Heroin has a long history. The first source was opium from poppies around 6000 BC; the Greeks recorded opium addiction in the third century BC. The Chinese first inhaled it in the 17th century. In 16th-century Europe, Paracelsus invented laudanum – an opium-based medicine that was used for painkilling and sedation well into the 19th century, until morphine was developed. A more powerful variant, diamorphine (heroin), appeared in Germany in 1874 and by the 1930s it had overtaken opium as the cheaper narcotic.

AROUND 200 PEOPLE EVERY YEAR IN THE UK

Heroin usage

Smoking heroin
- Known as "chasing the dragon" or "booting", this method is **far less dangerous** than injecting and gives a similar hit – it's intense and felt very quickly.
- Heroin is occasionally smoked in a pipe or hand-rolled cigarette, or heated from below on tin-foil.

Injecting heroin – the dangers
- Injecting directly into the vein is the **MOST DANGEROUS** way of taking heroin. It must be made into a liquid first. China white and pharmaceutical heroin will dissolve in water. Brown has to be dissolved in an acid – dissolved vitamin C powder is the least dangerous.
- Dissolving crushed tablets is even worse. It leaves undissolved grains that cause blockages in small blood vessels, leading to **abscesses and infection**. To try to prevent this some users draw the liquid into a syringe through a cigarette filter – this doesn't make it safe.

Hygiene
- The syringe and any other paraphernalia (the works) must be sterile – and a fresh needle used every time
- Used needles should be disposed of safely – never leave them lying around.
- Needle exchanges supply sterile needles. Local health authorities or the National Drugs Helpline will have details of the nearest needle exchange.

Never share someone else's works – that's how infections like HIV/AIDS and hepatitis B and C are spread.

"I've been on smack for 10 years. It's changed me completely. I'm anti-social, I'm ill, I'm shoplifting and doing burglaries. Of course I wish I'd never got into drugs."

WARNING! Heroin can kill at any time because the purity varies and you can never be sure what's in it.

Speedballs
Don't on any account take a "speedball", a mixed injection of heroin and cocaine. It's **very dangerous** as the two drugs worsen each other's effects.

THE COMFORT FROM HEROIN IS TEMPORARY

A smack in the face

OVERDOSING If you're not used to taking heroin, overdosing is a real possibility – especially if you're injecting. When you've overdosed, your breathing slows right down and breaths become so shallow that your body doesn't get enough oxygen. **Unconsciousness** follows and if you don't get to a hospital quickly, **your breathing may stop altogether** and you'll die.

NAUSEA AND VOMITING First-time users could easily be sick and if you pass out, there's a real risk that you could **choke on your vomit**.

SELF-NEGLECT If you're an addict, heroin quickly becomes the only thing in your life. You lose weight and **become malnourished** because you don't eat, and you **look even worse** because you can't be bothered to wash. But you won't care about any of this – getting your next hit will be the only thing that matters.

ABSCESSES, SORES AND OPEN WOUNDS With heavy use, these develop at injection sites – they're **unattractive** and very PAINFUL

Crime Often the only way to pay for a habit is to steal, and addicts will steal from just about anywhere. Some are so **desperate** they even steal from their own families. Crime only leads to one place – **prison**.

Never mix heroin with other drugs. Heroin is so powerful on its own that the addition of any other drug can kill.

Stay out of trouble

Heroin is **dangerous**: you can't guarantee your safety, but the risks can be lowered.

Don't inject Smoking provides a similar hit and is far safer. NEVER share needles.

Don't leave needles lying around Dispose of them safely.

Know what you're taking There's no time for regrets if you overdose.

Don't top up You'll overdose.

Know your limits Tolerance drops if heroin isn't used for a while, so a "normal" quantity could kill.

Be sensible Don't drive, ride a bike or use machinery while on heroin.

Practise safe sex There's even more reason to use a condom because of the high incidence of HIV/AIDS among users.

– REALITY WILL SOON HIT HARD

Signs of addiction

You're on a slippery slope if:

- you find it hard to get to sleep
- you get pains in your muscles
- you feel very sick and constipated.

Heroin and addiction

Heroin is **severely addictive**: users can develop a physical and psychological dependency on the drug, despite having been sure they could stay in control. The less stable and good your life is, the greater the chance of becoming addicted to the warmth and detachment from reality that heroin brings.

No excuses

Some people blame their dependency on their "addictive personality". There's no such thing: it's just an excuse to avoid looking at the real reasons behind their drug dependency.

What it's like to be addicted

- Your body needs heroin just to feel normal.
- Your *physical craving* becomes so strong that your whole life revolves around finding the money and the drugs for your next hit.
- The *psychological craving* is as strong as the physical. **You're terrified of being without heroin.** You end up more fearful o life and more isolated with a heroin habit tha you ever were before you got one.

Heroin tolerance

Users quickly gain a tolerance to heroin so the body learns to cope with it and needs more to feel the original euphoric rush.

- Eventually, it can get to the stage where even high doses merely take away the pain and craving – there is no euphoria.
- BUT if you stop using heroin, tolerance falls quickly. If you start again, your body won't be able to cope with the same amount and you could overdose.
- Smoking heroin keeps tolerance at a more even level than if it's injected.

The Law

Heroin is a Class A drug. It's illegal all ove the world and having, using or supplying it are seen as very serious offences everywhere.

- The penalty is sometimes a very long prison sentence and a fine.
- In some countries, possessing or supplying heroin may even carry the death penalty.

IF YOU KEEP AWAY FROM HEROIN, YOU'LL NEV

Cold turkey

Heroin withdrawal is bad. Users who suddenly stop will suffer psychological and physical withdrawal symptoms, which come on quickly. This means:
- intense psychological craving
- panic attacks
- inability to sleep
- nausea and diarrhoea
- sweating
- hot and cold flushes
- stomach cramps
- muscle and joint cramps
- inability to get comfortable.

It sounds like torture, but it won't be as nightmarish as you think. Fear of withdrawal is why many users avoid coming off the drug.

Kicking the habit

If you're dependent on heroin, it'll be difficult to come off it. BUT it isn't a lost cause. **Many people have given it up – you can too.** First you've got to accept certain things:
- only you can do your detox – others just help
- you have to want to come off
- do it for yourself – nobody else matters.

DETOXIFICATION

No-one should kick heroin by themselves; if you or someone you know has a heroin habit, **get professional help.** Remember that all drug agencies and medical services will treat your case in complete confidence. The first few days are the hardest. Once you're through them, hang in there. You've got this far, you can pull it off.

STAYING OFF HEROIN

This is the toughest part.

Keep busy Get a job or do community work. Take up hobbies.

Stay away from anything that reminds you of heroin Steer clear of other users and places where there are drugs.

Get support When your will-power is slipping, talk to someone: friends, family or professional drug organizations.

■ ■ IF SOMETHING GOES WRONG ■ ➡

Hitting an artery

If you hit an artery when injecting, staunch the flow of blood by applying firm pressure over the injury, holding the limb as high as possible.

☎ **Call an ambulance** or go straight to the hospital Accident and Emergency department.

unconsciousness

If your friend is breathing, place her in the recovery position (*see page 120*).

☎ **Call an ambulance.** Tell the medical staff what your friend has taken – it could save her life.

- Be prepared to resuscitate your friend if she stops breathing (*see page 121*).
- If your friend is sick while unconscious check that she's still breathing.

If in doubt, phone the National Drugs Helpline 0800 776600

AVE TO SWEAT OUT THE PAIN OF WITHDRAWAL

METHADONE

Street names

Dolly, Doll, Red Rock, Phy-Amps, PHY

What is methadone?

Methadone is a man-made chemical that has similar properties to opiates such as heroin. **Most of the information on heroin goes for methadone as well**. It's often used by doctors to wean addicts off heroin on a controlled regimen.

The methadone effect

The effects of methadone are similar to heroin, but it's not as powerful.

• **There's no intense hit**, which is why heroin users don't like it as much.

• The effects are longer lasting than heroin – PAIN RElief and feelings of well-being can last up to 24 hours.

What you won't like

You may also suffer from nausea and vomiting, severe constipation, stomach and back pain and loss of sexual drive.

form

• Methadone comes as tablets and ampoules of clear, injectable liquid. Both are prescribed under the trade name Physeptone.

• It's also found as a brown, orange or green linctus of varying strengths or as a mixture known as DTF, which comes in the same colours as the linctus, but is stronger.

Don't inject – injecting anything is stupid!

There's a risk of **overdose** and, if you share needles, of getting infections like HIV/AIDS and hepatitis B or C.

Methadone and other drugs

Some people have started using methadone to help them come down from ecstasy and amphetamine. It's true that this will take the edge off a comedown but it's an **extremely dangerous** way to do it. The abrupt change to your heart-rate puts your heart under great stress; if you don't know what you're doing you may take too much or mix it with dangerously high levels of other depressants such as alcohol or tranquillizers. The net result is your heart-rate and breathing slow so much they could stop completely.

METHADONE MAY BE A LEGALLY PRESCRIBE

Addiction

Methadone is **as addictive as heroin**. You can quickly gain a physical and psychological dependence to methadone if you use it regularly and this can be as strong as heroin dependence.

Methadone tolerance

This builds up with continued use, although not as quickly as with heroin.

• Because methadone is chemically similar to heroin, methadone tolerance can be transferred to heroin and vice versa.

• Methadone tolerance is quickly lost. If you don't use it for a week, your tolerance will be back to near zero. So if you take your "normal" dose again it can result in an overdose.

Withdrawal

Methadone withdrawal is **even tougher than heroin withdrawal**.

• If you're trying to come off methadone, you must get **professional help** because your dose needs to be brought down gradually over a period of a few weeks.

• The physical and psychological effects can be as bad as for heroin, but the real problem is that the withdrawal symptoms can last for six weeks or more. However, the pain and fear will gradually reduce after the struggle of the first 2–3 weeks. **No matter how hard it is, remember that people have done it before you.**

The Law

Methadone is a Class A drug, but it's schedule 2 which means it's only legal to have if it's prescribed for you by a doctor. It's illegal to give it away or sell it to someone else.

Methadone and clubbing

Never use methadone to come down after you've been clubbing. One ex-clubber, who is now a methadone addict, says: "Lesson no 1: don't take fast drugs [such as ecstasy] followed by slow drugs [such as methadone] because your heart can't take it and just 20 ml of the stuff could kill you."

SAFETY

As with heroin, you can't guarantee your safety on methadone but you can lower the risks. Most importantly, don't mix it with other drugs.

IF SOMETHING GOES WRONG

unconsciousness

If your friend is breathing, place her in the recovery position (*see page 120*).
☎ **Call an ambulance.**

Tell the medical staff what your friend has taken – it could save her life.

• Be prepared to resuscitate your friend if she stops breathing (*see page 121*).

• If your friend vomits while unconscious, check that she's still breathing.

If in doubt, phone the National Drugs Helpline 0800 776600

LTERNATIVE TO HEROIN BUT IT'S JUST AS DANGEROUS

What is acid?

Acid (LSD or **L**ysergic acid **d**iethylamide) is an extraordinarily powerful, **mind-altering drug**, meaning that it affects your brain, causing **hallucina**tions that alter how you perceive the world and make images more *intense*.

Street names
Trips, Tabs, Blotters, Microdots

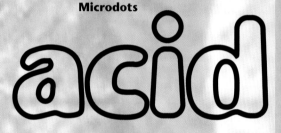

form

ACID is a transparent crystal in its pure form, but you won't find it like this. Acid is almost always soaked into small squares of blotting paper, called tabs, blotters or pieces.

• TABS come in sheets of over a hundred. Each tab is about 5 mm square and has a picture or design on it that varies according to fashion (strawberries and penguins are just some that have been

used). A small square of paper, whatever the picture, is pretty much a guarantee that it'll be acid.

• MICRODOTS are small coloured pills that have been impregnated with acid, but they're not as common as tabs. They're only 2–3 mm across and can be different colours. They often contain high doses of acid.

Brief history

The hallucinogenic properties of LSD were discovered in 1943 by a Swiss chemist called Albert Hoffman, who was researching its use as a heart stimulant. He accidentally took 250 micrograms of LSD – about five times today's average dose! Hoffman said it was terrifying; at one point he thought he'd died because he had an out-of-body experience. In the 1960s, a US professor, Timothy Leary, began experimenting with hallucinogenic drugs and encouraged a whole generation to follow his tips for trippy enlightenment.

Quantity

The average amount in an acid tab is around 50 micrograms, enough to induce a fairly mild trip. But a tab or dot could contain anything from 25 micrograms to 250 micrograms – enough to make someone temporarily deranged or cause the equivalent of a nervous breakdown.

A BAD TRIP IS A TERRIFYING ROLLER-COASTE

The acid effect

The effects of acid start about 30 minutes after taking it, peak after about two hours and may stay like that for several hours, until the user falls asleep. When people are on acid it affects **what they see** on the outside and **how they feel** on the inside.

WARNING!
Just a single "full-bottle" acid can make you hallucinate for 12 hours – it's that powerful.

Set and setting

Acid is **unpredictable** and taking it needs careful planning. How you feel when you take it (the set), and where you are and who you're with (the setting) are crucial. Never take acid on the spur of the moment.

• If you're down, **nervous**, **anxious** or **upset**, you're far more likely to have a **"bad trip"**. If you're happy and r e l a x e d, you're more likely to have a **"good"** one.

• To lessen the chances of a bad trip, you need to be in a place that won't freak you out, with people who make you feel at ease. Don't take acid in an environment you can't control – taking acid in a club is a very bad idea. Once on a bad trip, you can't come off.

The external world

Acid alters people's perception of the world around them:

• the **brightness of light fluctuates**
• sounds shift from loud to quiet and vice versa
• colours become more VIVID
• textures feel different – smooth feels jagged and vice versa
• images start to change shape
• people **hallucina**te – see things that aren't there; sometimes these are pleasant, sometimes very unpleasant.

The internal world

Users feel a change in their conscious mind and start to look inside themselves.

• They may start to look at the world from a completely different perspective, asking themselves extraordinary questions and knowing the answers – **some people say they understand things as never before**.

• During a particularly intense trip, it's possible to have an **out-of-body experience**. This is when users see their body from the outside and their mind is completely detached. This can be extremely unnerving for someone who is not prepared for it.

What's a trip like?

• A **good trip** can be **mellow, thrilling and mind expanding**.

• A **bad trip** can be like a nightmare and can trigger a drug psychosis so **you can never quite escape the nightmares**. *AND a bad trip can happen at any time.*

What can go wrong

There's virtually no risk of physical side effects from taking acid and it's not addictive, but the mental effects can be very serious.

• You can quickly become paraNoid – you think everyone is out to get you, or laughing at you. If no-one reassures you, you'll spend the next few hours going from bad to worse.

• Because it's a **mind-altering** drug, acid can unlock a mental illness of which you weren't even aware. This can lead to you becoming depressed, paraNoid or even needing psychiatric treatment.

What happens on a bad trip

To get some idea of how **bad** a bad trip can be, **remember the intense fear just before waking up from a nightmare**. The hallucinatiOns that you experience while on acid can suddenly change from weird and funny to *terrifying*. The more you've taken, the greater the chance that this will happen. The danger comes from what you might do while on a trip.

• People have been known to try to "escape" from terrifying hallucinatiOns or severe paraNoia by literally running away. By doing so, they risk having an accident, such as running in front of a car or falling from a great height.

• People have believed they can fly, walk on water or stop traffic while on a "trip". They put themselves and other people at risk. These incidents are rare, but they have happened so **keep an eye on your friends**.

• Even when a bad trip is over, it's possible to suffer terrifying flashbacks for weeks, months or even longer.

Don't try to beat the trip – relax. Don't examine everything you do, wondering if it's normal or not – you'll send yourself spiralling into paranoia.
Don't take acid with other drugs. It increases the risk of sending you out of control.
Don't take acid on your own.
Don't take more acid once you've had some – a tiny bit more could be disastrous.
Don't take it if your mood is anything but relaxed and happy.
Don't drive a car, ride a bike, use machinery.
Don't take it if you have to be in a normal state in 12 hours' time. Sunday night is no time to take acid if you're due in to work or college on Monday morning.
Don't take acid if you don't know its strength.
Don't take more than a tiny piece the first time.

Acid can unlock mental disorders of which you're not even aware.

ACID IS SO UNPREDICTABLE YO

Flashbacks

Taking acid can have a very unpleasant long-term effect – **flashbacks**. Although they're rare, flashbacks can occur days, weeks, months, even years, after the original trip.

• Flashbacks can be terrifying, and often involve the same **hallucina**tiOns or feelings you experienced during the original trip.

• They're inescapable: they're shorter than the original trip, but they can go on for hours.

• **Anything can trigger a flashback** so you can't take precautions against them.

What to do if you get flashbacks

• Try to stay calm. Tell yourself that you're just reliving the trip and that it will end soon.

• If you're driving or operating machinery, stop.

• If you're in a noisy place, go somewhere quiet; the flashback will be easier to deal with.

Your worst nightmare

There is an infinite number of things you might perceive on a bad trip. Imagine looking at yourself in the mirror and seeing your face melt in front of your eyes, or your urine turning into blood. It looks real – and **YOU'LL THINK IT'S REAL.**

WARNING! A bad trip is usually due to too much at a bad time when you're in a bad frame of mind, but it could happen at any time.

The Law

LSD is a Class A drug, carrying the same penalties as cocaine and heroin.

• Having any amount for personal use could lead to a prison sentence and a fine.

• Supplying the drug or possessing the drug with intent to supply – whether you're giving it away or selling it – results in a prison sentence which could be for life, AND an unlimited fine AND seizure of drug-related assets.

➤ ➤ IF SOMETHING GOES WRONG ➤ ➤

Panic attack
If your friend is paranoid, anxious and starts to panic take her to a quiet room away from large groups of people and try to reassure her. Offer her a hot drink or some water, and keep talking to her. Don't let her wander off alone. If your friend

begins panting (hyperventilating), get her to try to breathe normally by copying you.

BAD TRIP
Your friend may begin to see or hear frightening things that aren't really there – this is known as hallucinating. This can be

extremely frightening and may cause your friend to panic. Talk to him and reassure him that the things he can see or hear are imaginary and will soon pass. Stay with your friend until the bad trip is over – don't let him wander off alone.

If in doubt, phone the National Drugs Helpline 0800 776600

:AN LOSE CONTROL IN A SECOND

What are magic mushrooms?

Magic mushrooms are **similar in effect to acid** as they contain chemicals that can trigger hallucinatiOns. They're wild mushrooms (fungi) from two main plant groups: the psilocybe group and the amanita species. Both types grow wild in the UK, but the most common is the Liberty Cap, which contains the hallucinogen psilocybin. Far harder to find is the Fly Agaric, which contains ibotenic acid – another hallucinogenic chemical.

Street names
Shrooms, Mushies

magic mushrooms

Magic mushrooms usage

• Both fresh and dried mushrooms are eaten raw, cooked or they're boiled up into a mushroom tea. But be warned – they don't taste very good.

• Dried mushrooms are smoked in a rolled cigarette or pipe.

form

Liberty Cap
A small pale yellow to light brown fungus with a slender stem and conical cap. Liberty Cap mushrooms grow abundantly in early autumn on open grassland, parks and roadside verges.

Fly Agaric
A larger bright red mushroom with white spots and a thick white stalk that grows in undisturbed woodland and is found in early autumn.
   Once picked, the mushrooms are usually dried to preserve them. The

Liberty Cap is dried whole and the pale cap darkens to brown or black. The dried cap of the Fly Agaric is cut into sections and the dried lumps turn brown. Once dried, both types are difficult to distinguish from other mushrooms.

The mushroom effect

How people are affected depends on their own tolerance and the strength of the mushrooms. There's usually no effect for the first half an hour. Some users have been known to eat more because they haven't started **hallucina**ting straightaway, but this can lead to real trouble. The effects usually peak after about three hours, and the whole experience can last for nine hours or more. Provided too many mushrooms aren't taken, a mushroom "trip" generally follows certain lines:

• users will feel happy and *euphoric*; they may get the giggles and find everything hilarious
• they feel detached from the world, and on a different wavelength to everyone else
• people become Excited and engrossed in whatever they're doing
• some begin to see and hear things that aren't really there (hallucinate). Sounds and colours may become distorted or *intense* and things may change shape (the psychedelic effect)
• users may lose track of time
• some people say they feel things on their skin that aren't there
• some experience a spiritual journey and a sense of **spiritual enlightenment**.

Set and setting

When taking any **hallucino**genic drug the set (how people feel when they take it) and setting (where and with whom they take it) are very important in determining whether or not the experience is a bad one.
• If you're worried or anxious, mushrooms can give you a scary shock. So, if you're going to take mushrooms, take them with people you feel comfortable with, in a place where you feel in control – don't take them at a big party or at a club with lots of strangers around you.
• Be aware of your mind-set. **If in doubt, don't take mushrooms** – you could spin off into an hallucinogenic paranoia.

WARNING! It's impossible to predict the effect of even one mushroom.

How much is taken?

As with all other drugs, no-one ever really knows how strong they're going to be; it depends on the size and age of the mushrooms and how they've been stored. Fly Agaric is much stronger than Liberty Cap, so it's impossible to predict how many mushrooms will bring on hallucinations; they affect different people in different ways. Remember, **once a "trip" has started, it can't be stopped**.

HANCE OF TERRIFYING HALLUCINATIONS

A bad trip

If you take mushrooms when you're not in the right frame of mind, you could end up having **a very nasty time**:

• feelings of paranoia can make you hysterical
• the **hallucina**tions can be ***terrifying*** and impossible to stop
• you may start to ***panic*** and become completely out of touch with everything and everyone around you. You'll be overcome with fear, **you can no longer control the drug – it now controls you**.

> WARNING!
> As a mind-altering drug, magic mushrooms can unlock mental illnesses of which you weren't even aware.

Brief history

Ancient peoples are known to have taken mushrooms to experience altered states of consciousness and gain spiritual enlightenment. For centuries, South American Indians have been taking a related drug – mescalin – derived from magic mushrooms. Aldous Huxley described taking mescalin with South American Indians in his book *The Doorways of Perception* (1935). It wasn't until the 1960s that Western cultures started to use mushrooms as a natural alternative to acid.

Poisonous mushrooms

Many people feel **sick** and di**zz**y and become anxious and scared the first time they take mushrooms because they're worried they've been poisoned. Starting out feeling this way will guarantee you have a bad experience. However, there is a real danger of taking a poisonous variety by mistake. There are several species that look very similar to Liberty Cap and Fly Agaric, and when mushrooms are dried only an expert can tell the difference. The dangers cannot be overstressed. The symptoms can take up to 40 hours to develop:

• some mushrooms cause stomach pains, vomiting and diarrhoea
• other poisonous mushrooms can cause respiratory failure, unconsciousness and death.

ONCE THE TRIP HAS STARTED

Avoiding the nightmare

You may be able to avoid a nasty experience on mushrooms if you **try to stay in control**. This is a fine line, so stick to the guidelines:

• **don't take too much.** A few too many mushrooms can have a very profound effect. You can't be sure of their strength or the way you'll react

• **don't mix mushrooms with other drugs**. You can't predict the effects of a drugs cocktail – and if they're bad, they'll be really **bad**

• **know what you're taking**. Try to find out where the mushrooms came from, although this isn't always possible. **As with all drugs, never accept them from a stranger**, even if they seem like the genuine article.

The Law

There are no legal restrictions on Fly Agaric mushrooms. Liberty Caps are not illegal if they're raw. But once prepared for use in any way – even by just drying them – they're regarded as a Class A drug. The penalty is a fine and prison for possession, and possibly life imprisonment, a fine and seizure of drug-related assets for supplying.

◀ ■ ■ IF SOMETHING GOES WRONG ■ ➡

panic attack
If your friend is paranoid, anxious and starts to panic take her to a quiet room and try to reassure her. Offer her some water, and keep talking to her. Don't let her wander off. If your friend begins panting (hyperventilating), get her to breathe normally by copying you.

Bad trip
Your friend may begin to see or hear frightening things that aren't really there – this is known as hallucinating and may cause your friend to panic. Talk to him and reassure him that the things he can see or hear

are imaginary and will soon pass. Stay with your friend until the trip is over.

Stomach pains, vomiting and diarrhoea

If you or a friend experience the above symptoms after eating poisonous mushrooms, ☎ **call an ambulance** or go to the nearest hospital. If one of you has vomited, give the doctors a sample of the vomit and of the mushrooms you've taken, if there are any left, to help them counteract the effects.

Difficulty breathing
Try to get your friend to lie in the recovery

position (*see page 120*) and ☎ **call an ambulance.** Keep checking his breathing and be ready to resuscitate (*see page 121*).

unconsciousness
If your friend is breathing, place her in the recovery position (*see page 120*).

☎ **Call an ambulance.** Tell the medical staff what your friend has taken – it could save her life.

• Be prepared to resuscitate your friend if she stops breathing (*see page 121*).

• If your friend vomits while unconscious, check that she's still breathing.

If in doubt, phone the National Drugs Helpline 0800 776600

HERE'S NO STOPPING IT

What is PCP?

The proper name for PCP is *phencyclidine*. Like ketamine, it was originally designed to be used as an **anaesthetic**, but because it caused confusion and delirium its use was abandoned. PCP is now only used on animals and even then rarely. Some PCP users may be unaware they have taken the drug because it's sometimes a hidden ingredient of ecstasy and cannabis resin.

Street names
**Angel Dust,
Elephant
Tranquillizer,
Rocket Fuel,
Zombie, Whack,
Embalming Fluid**

Safety

• Never take PCP with other drugs.
• Don't take PCP when you're out clubbing.
• Don't take PCP if you have a history of mental illness.
• **Never inject**.

form

PCP is a white, impure, crystalline powder. It's swallowed, snorted, smoked or – rarely – injected. Sometimes it's mixed with cannabis and tobacco and smoked like a joint, or occasionally as skinny brown roll-ups that have been dipped in liquid PCP.

The PCP effect

Depending on how it's taken, the effects start in anything from a matter of seconds to about half an hour afterwards. There's a lot going on in the mind and body – it's said to be like taking amphetamine and acid, and drinking alcohol all at the same time.

• PCP acts as a **stimulant**, increasing body temperature, causing palpitations and **boosting energy and confidence**.
• But it also acts as a **depressant**, causing drowsiness, slurred speech, muscle rigidity and **lack of co-ordination**.
• On top of that, the **hallucinogenic** effect makes the user see and feel things that aren't really there. It can give a weird "out-of-body" experience and **distort**ed body image.
• Because users lose their inhibitions and have a reduced sensitivity to pain, they often become **AGGRESSIVE** and **violent**.
• PCP also releases adrenaline so users become immensely **strong**; if they become obstreperous they often need several people to control them – and that means the police.

PCP IS A NASTY, VICIOUS DRUG THAT CA

Horrors

PCP isn't addictive, but it's a **horrible drug** that can cause blurred vision, inability to speak or move, nausea, vomiting, memory loss, hallucinations and dehydration.

• If you're susceptible, your muscles may go into spasm and you could end up in a **coma**.

• People have **died** from prolonged fits (convulsions), a heart attack and even ruptured blood vessels in the brain as a direct result of taking PCP.

• There's a risk of **permanent mental derangement** from long-term use.

The long way down

A PCP comedown is one of the worst. It can go on for days with alternate periods of sleeping and wakefulness, followed by memory loss of the whole episode. The after-effects of one dose can last weeks, even months, with **anxiety, panic attacks, paranoia and depression.**

Flashbacks

PCP is stored in the body's fat cells, and therefore can never be completely eliminated. So if you take exercise or dance a lot, the drug in the fat cells will be stirred up again and your bad trip can come back, with hideous flashbacks.

The Law

PCP is chemically related to ketamine and has the same legal status. This means that it's not controlled under the Misuse of Drugs Act and it's not illegal for an authorized person to possess it. However, its sale and supply are controlled under the Medicines Act and it's illegal to give it away or sell it.

IF SOMETHING GOES WRONG ➡

FITS

Ease your friend's fall and clear a space around her. Loosen clothing around her neck and put something soft under her head. When the fit stops, put her in the recovery position (*see page 120*).
☎ **Call an ambulance.**

Bad trip

Your friend may see or hear frightening things that aren't really there – this is known as hallucinating. Talk to him and reassure him that the things he can see or hear are imaginary and will soon pass. Stay with your friend until the bad trip is over.

unconsciousness

If your friend is breathing, place her in the recovery position (*see page 120*).
☎ **Call an ambulance.** Tell the medical staff what your friend has taken – it could save her life.

• Be prepared to resuscitate your friend if she stops breathing (*see page 121*).

• If your friend vomits while unconscious, check that she's still breathing.

If in doubt, phone the National Drugs Helpline 0800 776600

AMAGE YOU PSYCHOLOGICALLY FOR LIFE

What is DMT?

DMT (***dim**ethyl**t**riptamine*) is an **extremely powerful** halluCino geniC drug found in certain tropical plants. Most street supplies are a home-made synthetic equivalent.

Street names
**The Businessman's Trip,
The Businessman's Lunch**

DMT

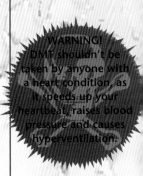

WARNING!
DMT shouldn't be taken by anyone with a heart condition, as it speeds up your heartbeat, raises blood pressure and causes hyperventilation.

form

• In its pure form, DMT is a white, strong-smelling crystal, but on the street it's normally a light brown powder. The powder or crystals are usually smoked through a glass or metal pipe. The powder can also be eaten.
• If it's prepared from the plant, it will generally be a greenish brown, thick sludgy liquid, which is difficult to swallow and then keep down. Raw leaves have no effect.

The DMT effect

The effective amount is higher than the amount taken for an acid trip, say, but this doesn't mean the trip will be lightweight. Take an average quantity and **the trip will walk all over any previous hallucinogenic experience.**
• If DMT is smoked, **the effects hit hard in a matter of seconds.** They'll peak after about five minutes, last for about 15 minutes and will be followed by a period of "cruise", similar to that experienced on a mild dose of acid.
• If DMT is eaten, the effects take about 2–5 minutes, peak after about 15 minutes and stay at that level for an hour or more.

WARNING!
DMT isn't for those who have psychological problems or those who aren't prepared to be terrified out of their brain.

The Law

DMT is a Class A drug controlled under the Misuse of Drugs Act. It carries the highest penalties for possession, use and supply.

What you won't like

DMT is **horrible**. It gives **an unpredictable, roller-coaster ride** involving a mixture of feelings – **euphoria, fear and insanity**.

• Once on the "trip", you can't get off it and it could feel like it's lasting for years.

• If DMT is smoked, the risks of a bad trip are even greater than if it's eaten.

Beyond that, the best way to describe the effects is to quote some people who've tried it:

"I got up and ran around, and when I did that everything started melting and I lost the outside world completely."

"I lay down, eyes open, and began to experience absolute terror. I was in a completely different universe – it was in no way similar to reality."

"There were snake-like things inside my legs, but at the time I didn't realize they were my legs."

"I knew I was insane, and I doubted I would ever recover. I didn't even know what being sane meant. I couldn't remember what it was like to be normal."

Words of advice

The DMT experience is very **intense** and not necessarily pleasant. The hallucinations are powerful and can be absolutely **terrifying**, and you can never really predict how you'll be affected. It doesn't seem to be as dependent on your mood as an acid trip – you might have a good experience one time and a **totally horrific** one the next. So if you take DMT, bear in mind the following:

• sit down or lie down when you take it – you'll almost certainly collapse if you're standing up

• never take it, unless you're with someone you trust

• choose a quiet, safe environment – a club is not the right place.

IF SOMETHING GOES WRONG ➤

Bad trip
Your friend may begin to see or hear frightening things that aren't really there – this is known as hallucinating and it may cause your friend to panic. Talk to her and reassure her that the things she can see or hear are imaginary and

will soon pass. Stay with your friend until the bad trip is over – don't let her wander off alone.

unconsciousness
If your friend is breathing, place him in the recovery position (*see page 120*).
☎ **Call an ambulance.**

Tell medical staff what your friend has taken – it could save his life.

• Be prepared to resuscitate your friend if he stops breathing (*see page 121*).

• If your friend vomits while unconscious, check that he's still breathing.

If in doubt, phone the National Drugs Helpline 0800 776600

REPARE YOU FOR THE EFFECTS OF DMT

What are tranquillizers?

Tranquillizers are **depressants**, which means they dull and slow down the central nervous system – **the opposite of stimulants** such as amphetamine and cocaine. Tranquillizers are prescribed for people who suffer from anxiety or those who have difficulty sleeping. Modern tranquillizers are based on the benzodiazepine group of drugs that largely replaced barbiturates in the 1950s.

form

There are many different brands of tranquillizer available on prescription. The following are just a few of the varieties favoured by illegal street-users:

Nitrazepam – "Mogadon" A long-acting (up to 12 hours) benzodiazepine hypnotic. It's an oval white tablet and was used as a sleeping pill in the 1970s and 1980s, but it's no longer prescribed in the UK.

Temazepam – "Normison" Another benzodiazepine hypnotic, but it only lasts 6–8 hours. It's legally prescribed in pill form, but gel capsules do turn up on the streets from abroad. Temazepam is one of the most commonly abused tranquillizers; it's sometimes used as a cheap alternative to heroin.

Diazepam – "Valium" A benzodiazepine anxiolytic, which means it reduces anxiety. It's a small white, yellow or blue tablet, of which white is the weakest and blue the strongest. It can last up to 24 hours.

Lorazepam – "Ativan" An anxiolytic like diazepam, but it only lasts 4–6 hours.

Street names
Tranx, Benzos, Blockers, Blockbusters, Chewies, Jellies, Eggs, Rugby Balls, Temazzies, M&Ms

TRANQUILLIZERS

DEPENDENCE ON TRANQUILLIZER

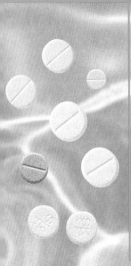

The tranquillizer effect

There are more bad points about tranquillizers than good ones in this profile. This isn't hiding the real facts from you – it's simply the truth. Benzodiazepine tranquillizers decrease your heart rate, lower your blood pressure and cause slow and shallow breathing. One tranquillizer per session or day **relieves stress and anxiety**, but can make the user feel drowsy. More than this may make the user feel:

- very **dopey**
- completely detached from any anxiety and stress
- **drunk, uninhibited and sociable**.

Going off the tracks with tranx

If you misuse tranquillizers by taking a high quantity, you'll encounter problems.

Extreme mood swings You may feel *euphoric* one minute, **irritable** and *AGGRESSIVE* the next.

Paranoia You'll think that everyone is against you, that they're laughing at you, excluding you or ganging up on you. Paranoia combined with a lack of inhibition can make you become aggressive towards people you wouldn't normally dream of hurting.

Hangover A night on tranquillizers will leave you with the **hangover to end all hangovers**. If you've been drinking or taking other drugs as well, it'll be even worse.

Depression Tranquillizers aren't called "depressants" for nothing. Long-term use can make you so **depressed** that you'll just want to hide away from the world. In this desperate state you're likely to become even more dependent on tranquillizers or other drugs.

Chronic fatigue You'll become so DRAINED of energy that you can't even eat or wash properly. You'll **lose weight** and *look terrible*.

Strange behaviour

A high quantity of tranquillizers can affect your judgement and make you act out of character. You're likely to take risks and do something stupid, such as shoplift or break into a car, because you'll believe you're invincible or even "invisible". The problem is that tranquillizers affect your judgement to such an extent that you're likely to be completely blatant about your behaviour and get caught.

AN HAPPEN VERY QUICKLY

A lethal injection

**WARNING!
More than one
tablet or capsule
could be dangerous,
especially if mixed
with other drugs.**

Some users take tranquillizers by grinding up the pills into a powder, dissolving it in water and injecting the liquid. Heavy tranquillizer users, and heroin users who can't get their habitual drug are more likely to inject the jelly-filled temazepam capsules.

Infection

Tranquillizers reduce your control and judgement, so **you're more likely to be careless when injecting**. You won't know whose works are whose, and you won't care anyway. All this makes the risk of being infected with HIV/AIDS and hepatitis B or C from shared needles and works even greater.

Vein blockages

Temazepam may give **a faster hit** when injected, **but there's a price to pay**. The liquified gel from the capsule can re-form once it's inside the veins so it's like injecting wine gums – **vein blockage can easily occur**, leading to abscesses, ulcers, blocked blood vessels and gangrene.

Overdose

There's always a greater risk of overdosing on a drug when you inject. **Once the drug is in your system it's too late to change your mind**. If you overdose on tranquillizers, your system slows down and eventually you could stop breathing, go into a coma and die.

The Law

The situation with tranquillizers and the law is complicated.
* *Some are Class B drugs, others are regarded as Class C.*
* *Some tranquillizers are legal to possess if they've been prescribed by a doctor, but illegal to supply. Others can be legal to possess without a prescription, but can't be supplied.*
* *Some only become illegal if they've been tampered with in some way for use. For example, if they've been prepared for injection they're regarded as Class A.*

**WARNING!
Don't drive
while on tranx.**

Tranx and alcohol

Tranquillizers minimize the control you have over your actions. Alcohol does the same. If you take them together, the combination can be lethal. Alcohol exaggerates the hypnotic effects of tranquillizers and can make you feel incredibly drowsy. This can then lead to all sorts of unpleasant and unpredictable problems:

• you could fall asleep, vomit, choke and die
• you could feel so spaced out that you accidentally overdose. You may just take a few more tablets and have another drink without thinking about the consequences. Eventually you'll slip into unconsciousness and could die
• alcohol also **intensifies** the anxiolytic effects of tranquillizers: anxiety and tension are greatly reduced so **you'll think you're indestructible**, and will end up getting into a fight. If you do, you'll be so unco-ordinated that you'll come off worse.

A risky way to come down

More and more people are taking tranquillizers to "chill out" after clubbing. This is a distinctly bad idea as **tranx and other drugs do not mix well at all**.

Staying out of trouble

DON'T take a stimulant, such as speed, to combat the chronic fatigue. The combination of a tranquillizer comedown and a speed comedown will leave you feeling even worse.

DON'T cross the danger line. The difficulty is knowing what a safe amount is, since the "safe amount" can still be very close to the danger line and, because of the nature of the drug, you can easily overdose without even knowing it.

DON'T drive, ride a bike or operate machinery. When you're on tranquillizers, you'll be in no state to do any of these things, even if you think you are. The same applies for the day after when you're struggling with a debilitating hangover.

DON'T be careless if you're having sex.

Despite what people say, tranquillizers are not aphrodisiacs, but they do lower your self-control, so you're more likely to have casual and unprotected sex.

DON'T take tranquillizers if you're pregnant. If you do, your baby may be born with a tranquillizer dependency and will have to go through withdrawal after birth.

ANGEROUS THAN INJECTING HEROIN

Tolerance

The body quickly develops a tolerance to tranquillizers. It learns to cope with the effects so you have to take a stronger dose more often to achieve the same effect. But, equally, if you stop taking tranquillizers for as little as a few weeks, your tolerance will reduce. If you then take what was your normal dose you're more likely to overdose because of the shock to your system.

Tranquillizer addiction

Physical and psychological dependence on tranquillizers can happen in an alarmingly short space of time. The higher the quantity and the more often you take them, the greater the chance of dependency. You reach a stage where **you can't cope without tranquillizers** and are terrified of trying to stop taking them.

Withdrawal

Suffering **withdrawal from tranquillizers is no joke**, but it can be done.
• Those who have gone through it say that it must be harder than coming off heroin.
• Sudden withdrawal is very DANGEROUS and potentially fatal. It can lead to paranoia, depression, panic attacks, shakes, waves of psychosis, hallucinations, nausea, insomnia and nightmares. These symptoms are particularly bad when coming off short-acting benzodiazepines, such as lorazepam.

If you're trying to come off tranquillizers you have to be weaned – so GET PROFESSIONAL HELP. Don't try to go it alone.

■ ■ *IF SOMETHING GOES WRONG* ■ ■

unconsciousness

If your friend is breathing, place her in the recovery position (*see page 120*).
☎ **Call an ambulance.**

Tell the medical staff what your friend has taken – it could save her life.
• Be prepared to resuscitate your friend

if she stops breathing (*see page 121*).
• If your friend vomits while unconscious, check that she's still breathing.

If in doubt, phone the National Drugs Helpline 0800 776600

IT'S VERY EASY TO CROSS TH

rohypnol

Street names
Roofies, The Forget Pill, Rochas, The Date-Rape Drug

What is rohypnol?

Rohypnol is a **powerful tranquillizer**. It's a relative of valium, only it's much stronger and **potently depressive**. Even a very small dose makes the user feel sleepy and dopey. Rohypnol is generally prescribed as a sleeping pill for severe insomnia, but it's also considered smart and hip by college girls on US campuses.

form
Usually white, easily crushable, odourless, soluble, tasteless tablets.

The rohypnol effect

One tablet is like drinking a six-pack of beer – and the effects can last up to eight hours.
• Just one tablet can make the user feel dizzy, **nauseous, feverish and disorientated**.
• More than one tablet will cause **instant drunkenness and memory loss**.
• One tablet can stop you breathing.
• Rohypnol plus alcohol can lead to **coma**.

How it's misused
Some users take rohypnol knowingly, but it's notorious for being used to **spike** the drinks of unsuspecting females. This way a man can have sex without the woman remembering or being in control of what's happening. The common scenario is of a woman at a party – passing out suddenly, being raped and having no recollection of what happened, sometimes for days.

The Law
Rohypnol isn't covered by the Misuse of Drugs Act, but it's a controlled drug under the Medicines Act. If any drug is given to another person without their consent (for the intention of having sex), this may be classed as rape or attempted rape and can result in a long prison sentence.

WARNING!
Rohypnol is fiendishly TOXIC to the liver.

IF SOMETHING GOES WRONG

unconsciousness
If your friend is breathing, place her in the recovery position

(*see page 120*).
☎ **Call an ambulance.**
Be prepared to resuscitate
(*see page 121*).

National Drugs Helpline 0800 776600

DANGER LINE WITH TRANQUILLIZERS

Street names
**Depressants,
Downers, Barbs,
Sleepers, Barbies**

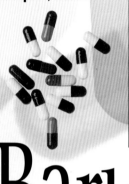

What are barbiturates?

Primarily hypnotic drugs, barbiturates like tranquillizers work by **depressing the nervous system**. In small amounts they calm you down and in higher amounts make you sleep. They belong to a 19th-century group of drugs and, until the 1950s, when safer alternatives were found, were prescribed for people who couldn't sleep or who had nervous disorders. Barbiturates are not without risks: they are **highly addictive and can suppress the function of the brain** to such an extent that breathing stops. The medical use of barbiturates is now limited.

BarbiturateS

How they work

Barbiturates depress the central nervous system so three main things happen to your body:
• the heartbeat slows down
• breathing slows down and becomes shallow so you don't take in much oxygen
• blood pressure falls.
It's the combination of these three things that makes barbiturates so **dangerous**.

form

Barbiturates come either as tablets or as gel capsules for swallowing. The most common forms seen today are:

Sodium amytal Bright blue capsules containing 60 mg of barbiturate.
Seconal Orange capsules containing 50 mg of

barbiturate.
Tuinal Blue and orange capsules containing 50 mg of amytal and 50 mg of seconal.

IT'S VERY EASY TO OVERDOS

The barbiturates effect

In the short term and in small quantities barbiturates **provide relief from insomnia, anxiety and tension**, and may make the user appear drunk. The effects can last for 12 hours or more, depending on the type and amount of barbiturate taken, the individual's tolerance and the circumstances in which the drug is taken.

"Barb freaks" are looked down on even by heroin users because of the totally desperate state they get themselves into.

Barbiturates are dangerous

There's a very fine line between the desired dose and the fatal one, which makes barbiturates **very dangerous**. Barbiturates give you an experience that is far from pleasurable:
• barbiturates won't make you feel euphoric or deliriously happy
• barbiturates won't make you chatty, sociable or sexy
• barbiturates will make you **a glazed-eyed zombie** that no-one wants to know
• barbiturates will give you a mind-numbing "hangover" the following day. You'll feel drowsy, unco-ordinated and **slow**.

WARNING! During the 1970s, 2000 people died every year from barbiturates – some did it on purpose, but others just wanted a good night's sleep.

WARNING! The safety margin with barbs is so small that you can overdose without knowing it.

DON'T INJECT

Some heavy users are foolish enough to dissolve the powder in water and inject it.
• If the powder doesn't dissolve properly it can cause vein blockages, which can lead to gangrene and amputation.
• The risk of overdosing on barbiturates is high anyway; if they're injected it's even higher.
• There's a risk of becoming infected with HIV/AIDS and hepatitis B or C from sharing needles and other equipment (works).

ACCIDENTALLY ON BARBITURATES

Long-term problems

You'll look awful Long-term use can lead to **depression** and intense tiredness, to the point where you can't feed or clean yourself properly.

Mood swings Heavy use may lead to unpredictable and extreme mood swings, often leading to **violent or strange behaviour**.

Bronchitis or pneumonia Both of these conditions may result from heavy use, and both can be **fatal**.

Hypothermia Barbiturates cause the blood vessels near the skin to dilate so you lose heat. With heavy use, your metabolism becomes so slow that **your body is unable to respond to the cold**. Hypothermia can be fatal.

WARNING!
Don't drive, ride a bike or operate machinery when using barbiturates. Even if you feel you can.

The Law

Some barbiturates are Class B, but more are Class C. This means that unless you have a valid doctor's prescription it's illegal to have barbiturates. In any event, it's illegal to give them away or sell them. Unauthorized possession or supply of Class B or C drugs can lead to a fine, prison sentence – or both.

Keep away from alcohol

It's suicidal to mix alcohol and barbiturates. Alcohol increases the effects of barbiturates as it too is a depressant drug. Here's the scenario:

• you've been out on the town, you've had a few drinks but decide it's time to wind down

• you take a couple of barbs, pour yourself one for the road and settle down

• half an hour later **your brain is so fuzzy yo can't even remember taking the pills**, so you have a couple more

• your heart-rate drops and your breathing gradually slows down until eventually you're not breathing at all – come the mornin you're dead.

WARNING!
The risk of overdose increases enormously if barbiturates are taken with alcohol.

Are they addictive?

Yes, barbiturates are **highly addictive**, both physically and mentally. They're even more addictive than drugs like heroin. After only a few days' use, you may be unable to go to sleep without taking them.

Withdrawal

Once you're addicted, withdrawal from the drug is horrible:
• you suffer severe *craving* for barbiturates – you can't live without them
• you suffer PAINFUL stomach cramps because your body needs barbiturates
• you may suffer fits (convulsions)
• you may suffer insomnia, depression, mental illness, *panic attacks* and **hallucina**tions
• you may even die, and not even heroin causes withdrawal deaths.

Tolerance

Because your body quickly learns to adapt to barbiturates, your tolerance increases. This means you need more to feel the same effects. If you don't use barbiturates for a while, your tolerance falls. If you then take what was a "normal" dose when you were a regular user, you could easily overdose.

Coming off barbiturates

If you're trying to come off, get professional help because your dose needs to be reduced gradually, and preferably in a hospital. Withdrawal will be bad, but it is possible to come off barbiturates.

IF SOMETHING GOES WRONG

unconsciousness
If your friend is breathing, place her in the recovery position (*see page 120*).
☎ **Call an ambulance.**

Tell the medical staff what your friend has taken – it could save her life.
• Be prepared to resuscitate your friend

if she stops breathing (*see page 121*).
• If your friend vomits while unconscious, check that she's still breathing.

If in doubt, phone the National Drugs Helpline 0800 776600

970s WERE DUE TO BARBITURATE OVERDOSES

What are sports drugs?

Anabolic steroids are the main sports drugs used to improve athletic performance. The *anabolic* part of the name means "promoting positive metabolism" – that is, increasing bulk. **Some people think that anabolic steroids on their own promote fast muscle development. They don't.** Strenuous exercise is required at the same time. Anabolics shorten the recovery time of muscles allowing a more rigorous regimen to be followed.

form

Anabolic steroids come as tablets, injections or implants. The most common types are Anavar, Sustanon and Dianabol.
Big is not better
Steroid drugs are prescribed in small quantities for very good medical reasons, but **it's a fallacy that what's good in small quantities is better in large amounts.** All body-building substances must only be taken under **strict medical supervision**, in small doses for short periods.

Why do people take them?

Many athletes and keep-fit fanatics are keen to excel in their field and develop the best body they can quickly. Some take sports drugs while they're training as a short cut to the body beautiful. It doesn't work – **any physical fitness gained is artificial and will disappear when they stop taking the steroids.**

The Law
Sports drugs are not controlled under the Misuse of Drugs Act. They are, however, controlled under the Medicines Act so they're only legal if they're prescribed by a doctor. It's always illegal to supply sports drugs to someone else or to manufacture them.

SPORTS DRUGS

Are steroids addictive?

Long-term users do experience cravings and withdrawal symptoms, but this may relate to psychological not physical dependency. Some people complain of feeling depressed. Others **don't seem to be aware that their body has changed**, even though it's obvious to other people, and because they don't think the drug is having an effect, they take more.

"Stacking"

When one anabolic steroid is combined with another or with recreational drugs, such as cocaine, it's known as stacking. **This can be fatal.**

Too high a price to look good

All sports drugs are **dangerous** and can leave you far from fit and healthy. Those peddled at gyms can be particularly dangerous because they're impure. Because anabolic steroids are derived from testosterone, they have dangerous androgenic side effects.

Physical effects Women become masculine (often irreversibly) with changes such as loss of breasts, a deep voice, excess facial and body hair, and infertility. Steroids can also cause **feminizing effects in men**, such as breast development. Anabolic steroids lead to acne, liver damage, raised cholesterol, heart attack, stroke, inability to maintain an erection and a lowered sex drive.

Psychological damage Users of anabolic steroids can become aggreSSive and paraNoid.

Injecting

When sports drugs are injected there's a real risk of OVErdose, and the danger of becoming infected with HIV/AIDS and hepatitis B or C from shared needles.

WARNING!
Misusing anabolic steroids before you've stopped growing can permanently affect your growth.

Other sports drugs

Amino acids The building blocks of protein, in high doses these are just as dangerous as anabolic steroids. They come as tablets or capsules – and because they're seen as "natural", 300 times the daily requirement is often taken. Taking too many amino acids can cause kidney failure.

Growth hormone (*L9H*) Responsible for healthy body growth, but only while you're growing. Once you've stopped growing, it can't make you any bigger, so instead it just distorts the body. Your hands, feet, jaw and face can become abnormally large, and your muscles get weaker, not stronger.

EPO (*erythopoietin*) Stimulates the formation of red blood cells, increasing the oxygen-carrying power of the blood and boosting stamina. Because it thickens the blood, it can cause a heart attack in a person who doesn't need it.

IF SOMETHING GOES WRONG

unconsciousness
If your friend is breathing, place her in the recovery position (*see page 120*).
☎ **Call an ambulance.**

Tell the medical staff what your friend has taken – it could save her life.
• Be prepared to resuscitate your friend

if she stops breathing (*see page 121*).
• If your friend vomits while unconscious, check that she's still breathing.

If in doubt, call the National Drugs Helpline 0800 776600

UIN A SPORTING CAREER

GETTING
HELP

Facing the facts

Admitting both to yourself and to someone else that
you have a problem with drugs takes guts, but it's
also the first step in successfully coming off a drug.
You don't have to face withdrawal alone; talking to a
friend or family member can provide crucial emotional
support, and getting professional help gives you the
necessary medical support. This chapter contains
practical advice to help you recognize when you have
a problem and know where to go for help.

As well as knowing how to help yourself, it's vital
to know when a friend has reacted badly to a drug
and how to help them. Learning the first-aid
techniques in this chapter will arm you with the
skills you need to deal with a problem.

DO YOU HAVE
A PROBLEM
WITH
DRUGS?

The warning signs that you could be getting into difficulties with drugs are identical to those of people who develop an alcohol problem. Such people:

- need a drink to face a tense situation
- need a drink to relax
- need a drink to go to sleep
- drink alone
- buy alcohol secretly
- stash alcohol secretly
- lie about how much they drink
- start to spend a lot of money on alcohol and steal if necessary
- panic if they run out of alcohol
- keep a 24-hour supply of alcohol
- can't start the day without a drink
- get the shakes if they don't drink.

Alcoholics have called this the slippery slope because as dependence on alcohol increases they care less and less about what it's doing and how it controls their life. At the bottom of the slope lies destitution (poverty, homelessness, solitude), serious illness and possible death. The slide down is inevitably accompanied by a steep decline into loss of self-esteem and self-confidence, which feeds the need for one more drink to blot out reality. This process is identical with other drugs.

Tolerance Your body needs the drug to feel "normal" and you need more and more to experience the same effects.

Addiction Physical craving becomes so strong that your whole life revolves around finding the money for your next fix, and then getting the drugs.

Dependence You become terrified of existing for even a day without drugs. You rely on the detachment from reality the drug brings, but relief is only temporary. You end up more fearful of life and isolated with a drug habit than you ever did before you got one.

Facing your problem

The climb up the slope is infinitely harder because it's all too easy to slide back down, especially if you gravitate towards people who are doing the same thing. Your "friends" at the bottom are almost exclusively drug takers and if you slide back, it's tempting to return to their company and revisit old habits.

Talk to someone else

It takes a great deal of courage to heed warning signs and accept that you could have a drug problem. But facing up to it is the first step in saving your future. The second step is harder – you have to admit your problem to someone else. You may find it easier to talk to someone who is neutral and understands – someone from one of the drug agencies, for example. The National Drugs Helpline (*see page 9*) can always help you to find your local drug agency. But you'll probably feel less alone if you can turn to someone who loves you and cares what happens to you. It could be your parents but it doesn't have to be. It could be your favourite teacher, an aunt or cousin, friend of the family or a grandparent. But the good thing about counsellors from drug agencies is that they've heard it all before – nothing you say will shock them, whereas you could shock someone who knows you well. What's important is that you're able to talk freely to whomever you choose. Your problem may seem insoluble to you but it only feels half as bad as soon as you tell someone. And there's a bonus. The person you've told will see the situation differently from you and is bound to

Needle users

If you've got to the point where you're injecting drugs, the chances are you've got a problem with drugs and you should get professional help. But in the meantime, be safe.

• Make sure syringes and other works are sterile, and NEVER use a needle twice.

• Dispose of used needles safely – NEVER leave them lying around. Put used needles inside the syringe and put them in a special **sharps box** so that no-one else can use them. This box has a one-way lid so you can put needles in but you can't get them out again.

• If you don't have a sharps box, get one. In the meantime, take out the plunger, put the needle inside the barrel and then press in the plunger. Then put the syringe into a sealed container, such as a drinks bottle, and take it to a **needle exchange**. A needle exchange provides users with a supply of sterile needles and sharps boxes. Phone the National Drugs Helpline for your nearest exchange.

• **Never** resheath needles: it can lead to confusion and potentially disastrous errors.

• **Never** use someone else's needle or other works; that's how infections such as HIV/AIDS and hepatitis B or C are transmitted between users.

come up with solutions or action plans that hadn't occurred to you. There's also an unexpected pay-off: you'll feel so good about facing up to your problem that your self-esteem will start to grow.

> *False...*
> *Some people take drugs because they have an addictive personality. There's no such thing. They're just using it as an excuse for not looking at the real reason behind their dependence.*

Kicking a drug habit

Coming off drugs is difficult and you shouldn't attempt to do it by yourself, but as long as you want to come off you can. Many people before you have come off drugs and if you go about it the right way and with the right help you'll succeed too. The fear of withdrawal often makes people imagine the worst possible scenario so they don't try to come off: they feel they can't face the struggle. **You have nothing to fear but fear itself.**

Getting help

Different areas have different schemes. Find out from the National Drugs Helpline (0800 776600) what services are available in your area; they can advise you on what type of help would be most appropriate. Alternatively, ask your GP to refer you to the most suitable

organization. Whatever you choose, remember that all drug agencies and medical services are duty bound to treat your case **in complete confidence**.

Coming off

Clearing your system can take anything from a few days to a few months, and for safety's sake it must be done under medical supervision. Some drugs can be stopped straightaway; others, like barbiturates and tranquillizers, have to be cut down gradually – to stop them suddenly is very dangerous. The first few days are the hardest, so once you're through them hang on in there – **it will get better, but it takes time.**

Staying off

Withdrawal is only half the battle: the toughest part is staying off the drug. Give yourself the best chance:
• keep yourself busy
• stay away from all drugs, and that includes alcohol
• avoid situations where there are drugs, and places where you used to go to take drugs
• avoid people who take drugs
• get support when it gets rough, when you feel you might slip back.

> *True...*
> *If you're going to beat drug addiction, first you need to be honest with yourself.*

WHAT TO DO IN AN EMERGENCY

Drugs are unpredictable – the same drug can affect different people in different ways. In an extreme case a friend may collapse unconscious after taking a drug. But a drug can also cause a person to become dangerously hot, very drowsy, have terrifying hallucinations or even have a fit.

CALLING AN AMBULANCE

Dial 999, ask for an ambulance and give the following information:
• the telephone number you are calling from
• where you are – the name of the club, for example
• what's wrong with your friend: she's very hot or she's collapsed; she's unconscious. Don't be afraid to say that your friend has taken drugs, and preferably name the drug: **the information could save her life.**
If someone else makes the call, ask him to come back and confirm that it's been done.

Take action

If a friend suffers adverse side effects from taking drugs, it may be frightening for you, but it could be life-threatening for your friend. It's vital to be able to recognize that something is going wrong as well as to know what to do in an emergency – **quick action can save lives.** Read the information given for each drug in the section "If something goes wrong". Also read and remember the procedures on the following pages and encourage your friends to do so as well. Better still, sign up for an accredited first-aid course.

Get help

• If you see someone you think has had a bad reaction to a drug don't hesitate to get help and **don't panic.**
• If you're in a club, shout for the security staff and ask for the qualified First Aider.
• If you're not in a club, ☎ **call an ambulance** or, better still, get someone else to make the call while you look after your friend.

FFECTS OF DRUG WITHDRAWAL

Has your friend collapsed?

YES

Does he respond if you shake his shoulders?

YES

NO

HE'S NOT UNCONSCIOUS
• Stay with him until he feels better.
• If he becomes very drowsy,

☎ CALL AN AMBULANCE.
Try to keep him awake while waiting for help.

HE'S UNCONSCIOUS
Open his airway
• Tilt his head back and gently lift his chin with your fingers. This stops his tongue falling back and blocking the airway and prevents him from choking.
• Shout for help.

THEN

Is he breathing?
• Kneel down and put your cheek close to his face.
• Can you feel his breath on your cheek, see his chest moving or hear him breathing?

YES

HE'S BREATHING
Put him in the recovery position
☎ CALL AN AMBULANCE.
• Stay with him and keep checking his breathing.

• If he vomits, clear the vomit away from his mouth and keep his head tilted back so that he can't choke.
• If he stops breathing, begin resuscitation (*see opposite*).

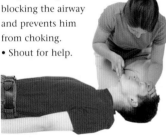

Make sure his head is tilted back

Keep his hand against his cheek

Keep his bottom leg straight

Bend his top leg into a right angle

Place back of his hand on the ground

HE'S NOT BREATHING
☎ CALL AN AMBULANCE
(ideally get someone else to call).
Begin mouth-to-mouth ventilation
– this means that you breathe into your friend's mouth to get oxygen into his lungs.

• Check that there's nothing in his mouth that might cause him to choke.

• Tilt his head back.

• Pinch his nostrils shut, seal your lips over his and breathe into his mouth; watch his chest rise and fall.

• Give another breath and then check the pulse on the side of his neck (*see right*).

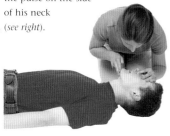

YES

THEN

Does he have a pulse?
• Put your index and middle finger on the side of his neck in the hollow between the Adam's apple and the neck muscle. Can you feel a pulse (the throb felt in an artery with each heartbeat)?

• If there is a pulse, continue mouth-to-mouth ventilation (*see left*), rechecking for a pulse every minute.

• If you can't feel a pulse, the heart has stopped beating and you need to start chest compressions (*see below*).

Use two fingertips to feel for the pulse

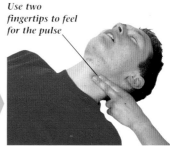

NO

HE HAS NO PULSE
Begin CardioPulmonary Resuscitation

Put fingers on lower breastbone

• Put your index and middle fingers on the lower breastbone (the bone where the ribs meet), and the heel of your other hand against the fingertips.

• Remove your two fingers from the chest. Put the heel of this hand on top of the other and interlock your fingers.

• Press down on the chest with the heel of your hand (to a depth of about 4–5 cm). Do this 15 times.

• Then give two breaths of **mouth-to-mouth ventilation** (*see above*). Repeat chest compressions and mouth-to-mouth ventilation until help arrives.

COMMON
DRUG
EMERGENCIES

VITAL INFORMATION

Tell the medical services what your friend has taken or, if possible, give them a sample of the drug itself. If your friend has vomited, keep a sample – it can provide vital information that could save your friend's life.

Panic attacks

Although panic attacks can be alarming, they're relatively harmless and usually pass. Panic attacks can happen if a person is having a bad trip on hallucinogenic drugs like acid or magic mushrooms, but they also come on with some cannabis blends and stimulants like ecstasy or amphetamine.

What are the signs?

• breathing is difficult, laboured, or far too fast

• sweating and trembling

• headache, backache, chest pains and palpitations

• difficulty swallowing.

What you can do

• Take your friend somewhere cool and quiet – the chill-out room if you're in a club.

• Try to reassure her and talk her down.

• Be firm, but don't shout at your friend or slap her.

• If her breathing is rapid and irregular, get her to breathe more slowly by copying your breathing.

Fits (convulsions)

Excessive amounts of alcohol and some drugs can trigger convulsions.

What you can do

• Clear the area around your friend.

• Loosen any tight clothing.

• Once the fit has passed, your friend may fall into a deep sleep.

• Check breathing, then put him in the recovery position (*see page 120*).

℡ **Call an ambulance.**

• Keep checking his breathing. If it becomes difficult or stops, be prepared to resuscitate (*see page 121*).

PASS ON ANY VITAL INFORMATIO

Dehydration/heat exhaustion

Stimulants like ecstasy and amphetamine raise body temperature. If a person then also dances for a long time without drinking enough, the body loses excessive amounts of fluid and salt. The result: heat exhaustion and dehydration.

What are the signs?

• complains of headache and cramp
• feels dizzy and faint
• looks pale and sweaty
• forehead looks flushed and feels very hot
• feels lethargic.

What you can do

• Take your friend to a cool place. If you're in a club go to the chill-out room and open the doors and windows.
• Lie her down and raise her legs.
• If possible, give her high-energy sports drinks, fruit juice or water to drink – **don't let her drink too much too quickly**.
• Remove any unnecessary clothing, splash her with water and fan her.
• If she doesn't improve or seems to be getting worse, ☎ **Call an ambulance.**

Severe bleeding

This is most likely to happen if a user hits an artery when injecting. It's very serious because a lot of blood is lost very quickly.

What you can do

• Preferably wearing protective latex gloves, place a clean pad over the wound and apply firm pressure to the area.
• Raise the affected limb as high as possible – above the level of the heart – to help slow down the blood flow.
• Secure the pad with a bandage if possible, keeping the pressure on the wound.
☎ **Call an ambulance.**

Drowsy, but conscious

If a friend becomes very drowsy as a result of taking drugs, it's important that he doesn't fall asleep. If he does, he could easily lose consciousness. Do everything you can to keep him awake while you're waiting for the ambulance to arrive.

What you can do

☎ **Call an ambulance.**
If you can't get anyone else to make the call, take your friend with you – don't leave him on his own.
• Keep him awake – talk to him, make him walk around, pinch him.
• If he's very thirsty, give him sips of lukewarm water (NOT black coffee).
• If you think that he's deteriorating, put him in the recovery position (*see page 120*). Keep talking to him to stop him losing consciousness.

USEFUL
ADDRESSES

ADFAM National
Tel: 0171 928 8900
Helpline providing free and confidential support and information to friends and families of drug users

AIDS Helpline
Freephone: 0800 567123
24-hour helpline for people with HIV/AIDS or for those who want information about the virus

Alcoholics Anonymous
(for England and Wales)
General Service Office of AA
PO Box 1
Stonebow House
Stonebow YO1 7NJ
Tel: 01904 644026/7/8/9
Fax: 01904 629091
www.alcoholic-anonymous.org.uk
Above phone number supplies general advice and local helpline numbers that provide confidential support for people who would like to talk about their drinking, and for concerned friends and families of drinkers

Al-Anon Family Groups
Tel: 0171 403 0888
Provides help and support for people who live with or have to cope with someone else's drinking problem

British Red Cross
9 Grosvenor Crescent
London SW1X 7EJ
Tel: 0171 235 5454
For information on first-aid training courses

Citizens Advice Bureau
National Association of
Citizens Advice Bureaus (NACAB)
115–123 Pentonville Road
London
N1 9LZ
Tel: 0171 833 2181
email: consultancy@nacab.org.uk
Free information on the legal issues pertaining to drugs

Cocaine Anonymous
Tel: 0171 284 1123
Helpline providing confidential advice and support for cocaine users

Drinkline
24-hour Freephone information line:
0500 801802
Provides confidential support and advice and gives information on local support groups

Drugs in School Helpline
Tel: 0808 8000 800
Information service for parents, pupils and teachers concerned about the use of drugs in school

Families Anonymous
The Doddington & Rollo
Community Association
Charlotte Despard Avenue
London
SW11 5JE
Tel: 0171 498 4680
Advice for friends and families of drug users; local support groups enable people to discuss and share their anxieties

Family and Friends of Drug Users
Tel: 01926 887414
Helpline providing advice and support for families and friends of drug users

Freephone Drug Problems
Dial-and-listen service giving details of drug agencies. Dial 100 and ask for the above

Health Education Authority (HEA)
Trevelyan House
30 Great Peter Street
London SW1P 2HW
Tel: 0171 222 5300
Provides leaflets and information on drugs

Institute for the Study of Drug Dependence (ISDD)
32 Loman Street
London SE1 0EE
Tel: 0171 928 1211
Fax: 0171 928 1771
email: services@isdd.co.uk
www.isdd.co.uk
Information and publications on all aspects of drugs

Kidscape
152 Buckingham Palace Road
London SW1W 9TR
Tel: 0171 730 3300
Fax: 0171 730 7081
National charity that teaches children how to avoid bullying and abuse and stay safe

Lifeline for Parents
101–103 Oldham Street
Manchester M4 1LW
Tel: 0161 839 2054
Fax: 0161 834 5903
email: drughelp@lifeline.demon.co.uk
Freephone: 0800 716701
Offers advice and counselling to parents who are concerned about their children's drug use

Narcotics Anonymous
Tel: 0171 730 0009
Free confidential counselling, advice and information

National Drugs Helpline
Tel: 0800 776600
Provides 24-hour confidential counselling for drug users; supplies free leaflets and literature on drugs and general drugs information

Rape Crisis Centre
PO Box 69
London WC1X 9NJ
Tel: 0171 837 1600
Helpline that offers confidential advice and support for rape victims

Release
388 Old Street
London EC1V 9LT
Tel: 0171 603 8654
email: info@release.org.uk
24-hour helpline that offers advice about drug abuse as well as information on the legal implications of taking drugs

Re-Solv
30a High Street
Stone
Staffs
ST15 8AW
Tel: 01785 817885
Fax: 01785 813205
email: re-solv@btconnect.com
Information and advice on all aspects of solvent abuse, from crime to health issues

Samaritans
Freephone: 0345 909090
email: jo@samaritans.org
www.samaritans.org.uk
Free, confidential service providing advice and support on any problem

Turning Point
London/South-East - Tel: 0171 702 1458
Scotland - Tel: 0141 418 0882
North - Tel: 0161 832 3417
Central/South-West - Tel: 0115 967 4777
Helpline that provides advice and support for a wide range of problems, from drug and alcohol abuse to mental health and learning disabilities

INDEX

The main drugs from the directory are in **bold** type.
The street names for each drug are in *italics*.

Acknowledgments

Nicky Adamson, Nick Casey – Substance Misuse Coordinator for East Sussex, Brighton & Hove Health Promotion, Fergu Collins, Sarah Coverdale, Anne Kramer: editorial assistance; Andy Crawford: additional photography; Tracy Beresford: proofreading; Hilary Bird: index.